All About Landscaping

Created and designed by
the editorial staff of
ORTHO BOOKS

Editor
Cedric Crocker

Writers
Alvin Horton
Lin Cotton

Illustrator
Frank Hildebrand

Designer
Gary Hespenheide

*Happy Mothers Day
1993
Love, Bev*

Ortho Books

Editorial Director
Christine Robertson

Production Director
Ernie S. Tasaki

Managing Editors
Michael D. Smith
Sally W. Smith

System Manager
Katherine Parker

National Sales Manager
Charles H. Aydelotte

Marketing Specialist
Susan B. Boyle

Operations Coordinator
Georgiann Wright

Circulation Manager
Barbara F. Steadham

Administrative Assistant
Kate Rider

Senior Technical Specialist
J. A. Crozier, Jr., Ph.D.

Address all inquiries to
Ortho Books
Chevron Chemical Company
Consumer Products Division
Box 5047
San Ramon, CA 94583

		7	8	9	
90	91	92	93		

ISBN 0-89721-150-2
Library of Congress Catalog Card
Number 88-71152

Chevron Chemical Company
6001 Bollinger Canyon Road, San Ramon, CA 94583

Acknowledgments

Additional Illustrations By
Wendy Bloom (page 75)

Copy Chief
Melinda E. Levine

Copyeditor
Judith Dunham

Layout By
Christine Dunham

Pagination By
Linda M. Bouchard

Editorial Coordinator
Cass Dempsey

Editorial Assistant
Karen K. Johnson

Proofreader
Susan Lang

Indexer
Frances Bowles

Art Director
Craig Bergquist

Production By
Studio 165

Separations By
Color Tech Corp.

Lithographed By
Webcrafters, Inc.

Special Thanks To
Harold Biswell, SAF Professor Emeritus,
 U.C. Berkeley
Wendy Bloom, landscape architect, Albany, Calif.
Bob Bryant
Jack Buktenica
E. Douglas Chism
Aylett and M. J. Cotton
David Davenport, Ph.D., U.C. Davis
Charles Deaton
Roger D. Fiske, Fiske Landscaping, Danville, Calif.
Randolph Ford, landscape architect, Mill Valley, Calif.
Fred Gilley
Ray Gustin III, Gustin Gardens, Gaithersburg, Md.
Steve Hanson
Ron Herman, landscape architect, Berkeley, Calif.
Jesse Lelianthal
Stephen Marcus
Phoebe Cutler Martensen
Garden pictured on pages 28 and 29 designed
 by Kathryn Matthewson Associates,
 San Francisco, Calif.
Oehme, van Sweden & Associates, Inc., Wash., D.C.
Theodore Osmundson-Fellow, ASLA
Ron Pryhuber
Roy Rydell, landscape architect, Santa Cruz, Calif.
Robert D. Steiner, AIA
Robert Tetlow, ASLA
Warren Thoma, Rain Bird Sprinkler Mfg. Corp.,
 Glendora, Calif.
Treetops Nursery, Albuquerque, N.M.
Robert Turner and Marguerite Viles, Santa Fe, N.M.
William Wilson
Betty Wood

Photo Editor
Roberta Spieckerman

Photographers
Names of photographers are followed by the page numbers on which their work appears. R = right, C = center, L = left, T = top, B = bottom.

William Aplin: 21B, 38, 46B, 53L
M. Baker: 17TR, 46T, 56B
Carol Bernson: 60T
Laurie Black: 36
John Blaustein: 30L
Tom Bradley: 51R
Richard W. Brown: 4
Josephine Coatsworth: 7, 40C, 55L, 58BL, 66, 67, 81L, 81R, 83T, 83B, 84T, 87B, 88B, 91T, 91B, 99, 103T, 103B, 104T, 104B, 105, 106T, 107, back cover TR and BL
Alan Copeland: 59T
Barry M. Friesen: Back cover BR
Saxon Holt: 14, 22TL
Susan Lammers: 63B
Michael Landis: Front cover, 8TR, 10B, 27TL, 30R, 31C, 31B, 45BR, 47T, 55R, 56T, 57L, 57R, 58BR, 82, 84B, 89, 92, 94B, 106B, 108C, 108B, 109, back cover TL
Michael McKinley: 6T, 6B, 10T, 11, 12, 13, 18B, 20, 24L, 24R, 26L, 26BR, 28, 32BL, 32BR, 33, 35BL, 35BR, 41, 45L, 45TR, 51L, 54, 59B, 60B, 61L, 63TR, 102R
James McNair: 17TL, 25L, 27BL, 42TR, 43, 63TL
Gary Mottau: 78
Douglas Muir: 1, 27TR, 27CR, 27BR, 64
Tom Tracy: 8TL, 26TR, 37, 39TR, 40T, 42TL, 44R, 47BL, 48, 52T, 52B, 53R
Ortho Photo Library: 8B, 9, 16, 18T, 19T, 19B, 21T, 22–23, 25R, 39TL, 42B, 44L, 47BR, 50, 56C, 58T, 61R, 62 (all), 102L, 108T

Front Cover
A well-conceived landscape makes the most of available space and does not always reveal its design.

Title Page
An attractive landscape invites the viewer to enter and enjoy it.

Back Cover
Various scenes of landscaping include (clockwise from upper right): creating working design plans, the completed landscape, installing a sprinkler system, and an aerial view of a landscape site.

All About Landscaping

Keys to a Good Landscape

A successful landscape is the result of the sensitive balancing of many elements. The first step is to decide exactly what you want and what you like, so that the finished landscape design will suit your tastes and needs.

All homeowners deserve a landscape that brings them pleasure and serves their needs. However large or small the yard or property, the life-style you enjoy inside your home can be extended to the environment outside your door. Thoughtful planning can yield a practical and enjoyable living space that only the outdoors can offer, whether you want to sunbathe, swim, play croquet or tennis, barbecue, work, dine in the shade, or just relax in a hammock.

Don't overlook the fact that a good landscape also increases the value of the property. The most important function of a landscape, however, is what it does for the people who live or visit there. The landscaped yard or garden should be a sanctuary, a place to discard worries and live with nature. It is in this landscape that you can putter, rest, eat, play, or just sit quietly contemplating the pleasures of the scene around you.

The advantages of having a beautiful landscape may seem obvious, but consider also the advantages of creating the landscape yourself. If you have ever thought about landscaping your yard, probably your first reaction was that you would need to call in the professionals and spend a great deal of money. The premise of this book is that landscaping is not mysterious. Anyone can learn to design a new landscape or improve an existing one, and can do it for far less money than hiring a professional.

The bench in this New England setting invites the viewer to relax and enjoy the garden.

WHAT IS LANDSCAPING ALL ABOUT?

Having decided you can do the landscaping yourself, you need to define just what it encompasses. A landscape is simply an outdoor environment, whether designed by nature or by people. The art of landscaping is the art of purposefully changing the natural features that exist out-of-doors, with the intention of making the environment more attractive or functional. Added features usually include plantings, as well as rock, wood, and other natural or man-made materials.

Landscaping may be considered a living sculpture, a work of art that changes with the seasons and grows with the years. Discard any notions about the right, or perfect, or ultimate landscape. The landscape should be distinctly your own, and there are as many possibilities as there are people and yards.

One of the traditions of Western civilization is the notion that your home is your castle and an expression of yourself. Most people want their homes and landscapes to have the colors, fragrances, furnishings, and spaces in which they feel comfortable.

In eighteenth-century England, landscaping was thought to be a form of art equal to painting, literature, music, and drama. Like these other arts, it was considered a unique mode of artistic expression. In formulating a landscape, you have the opportunity to express your own ideas and to put together a pleasing and suitable environment.

Natural Beauty

As with other artistic endeavors, as you plan, you may go beyond your immediate goals. You may experience the wonderful pleasure of creating natural beauty for its own sake, and in the process become attuned to nature's continuing cycle of life. In the Greek myth of the Minotaur, Theseus leaves for Crete to do battle with the monster Minotaur. His father, the king of Athens, afraid that his son will not return, goes out and plants trees. Because the king is an old man, people ask him why he has bothered to plant these trees, since, surely, he will not live long enough to see them grow to maturity. The king replies that he is planting trees for his son Theseus because, if Theseus is killed by the Minotaur, the trees will still grow and bear fruit, symbolically continuing

Above: A landscape can provide a sanctuary where worries may be left behind.
Left: Any outdoor space can be the setting for a landscape. This urban apartment balcony has been transformed into a cozy garden with container plants, a bird feeder, and wind chimes.

the life of his son. Recognizing the continuation of life in what we plant ties us to life forces far greater than our own lives. Planting living things and establishing places of beauty that will continue in the future, often beyond our lifetimes, can be a satisfying experience.

The Successful Landscape

The first hurdle in any project is getting started, and a big step toward jumping that hurdle is having confidence in yourself. One purpose of this book is to provide all the needed information so that you will develop confidence in your ability to create a successful landscape.

The key to a good landscape is design, as distinguished from mere decoration. To decorate is to put things into the environment without a purpose in mind. There is no real intent, no plan, no essential connection to you, the creator. When you design a landscape, you know why you are putting this plant here and that walkway there. A designed landscape is one that has been thought through, whose choices are conscious and intentional. Your landscape is an entire stage show, directed to please one audience: you.

Since a successful landscape does what you want it to, the place to start is with yourself. What do you like? What effects please you and make you feel good?

Think of a place you have been that you really loved. Perhaps it was your grandmother's garden, or a particular place in a park, or the deck or patio of a friend. Wherever it was, the special quality that you liked made you want to be there. The nature of those special places—the qualities they contained and the feelings you had when you were there—are all elements of landscaping. You will make a successful landscape to the extent that you can re-create these effects.

Establishing a place of beauty is one of the reasons for creating a garden.

But most of us do not have an idea of how to create these effects. To help develop an understanding of why certain effects are appealing, begin a scrapbook or a file of ideas that appeal to you. Fill it with notes made from memory, pictures from books and magazines, photographs of gardens passed on the street, clippings from newspapers—any and all sources. The point is to assess all the landscaping ideas that are pleasing to you. The clearer you are about what you like, the easier it will be for you to create those qualities in your own landscape.

THE PURPOSE OF THIS BOOK

This book will assist you in the designing and building of a landscape that expresses your tastes and interests, takes into account your particular environmental assets and problems, and meets your practical needs. The first five chapters contain information on landscape design, which goes beyond that of the standard how-to landscape manual. By understanding the qualities that make a landscape work, you will not be forced to mold your yard into Landscape Plan A, B, or C, none of which may incorporate your favorite ideas or style or be suitable to the setting.

At any stage along the way, it may be necessary to get professional assistance. What

Above: Natural stone, an arched bridge, and native plants highlight the natural force of this setting.
Opposite, above left: High above a busy street, this garden oasis is virtually unnoticed by neighbors and passersby. Careful screening out of a neighboring apartment and the preserving of the open view have created a pleasant, sunny spot to enjoy nature.
Opposite, above right: Relaxation can be an important part of enjoying the garden.
Opposite below: This vegetable garden is both practical and visually appealing.

you prefer to do yourself and what you want to leave to others depends largely on your interests, skills, available time, energy, and budget. If you mainly want to pursue aspects of design and planning, this book will provide the necessary insights and information and will help in selecting and supervising contractors for planting and construction.

On the other hand, if you want to do the planting and construction yourself and obtain professional help with the design, this book will provide basic construction information and give a good basis for consultations with a landscape architect. One of the landscape architect's tasks is to help you select the exact effects you want. By doing some of the preliminary thinking yourself with the aid of this book, you can use an architect to help you expand and refine the ideas you have already come up with, thereby saving time and money, and probably frustration.

On the other hand, if you wish to do everything yourself, from start to finish, this book will help you to do just that.

THE PLAN OF THIS BOOK

The rest of this first chapter is devoted to some general, but important, concepts intended to expand your view of what is possible in the creation of a landscape.

The second chapter, "Landscape Style," discusses some basic concepts of style in landscape design and illustrates a selection of landscape styles. Style is usually the first element you notice about a landscape. The overall statement that a landscape makes is a separate issue from fundamental design principles, such as enclosure and space. Considering elements of style and looking at examples of a range of styles will allow you to distinguish between style and design and to identify the features of landscapes that you like.

Basic design principles are covered in the third chapter, "The Elements of Design." These are the very specific forces of a landscape: fragrance, color, light, texture, and sound. Understanding the elements that are present in every good landscape, regardless of its style, will make it possible to analyze what you admire in the landscapes that attract you. A knowledge of these fundamental design principles will enable you to manipulate them into the landscape effect you desire.

Plants and materials make up the landscape designer's palette. Selecting them carefully is an essential step in forming a landscape. The fourth chapter, "Plants and Materials," identifies the particular features of plants and construction materials that you should consider when making your choices.

After familiarizing yourself with basic design considerations, begin to set a plan down on paper. By answering a series of specific questions, you can gather your ideas and start to order your priorities. Then, with the information in the fifth chapter, "The Design Process," commit your plan to paper. Try anything from freehand thumbnail sketches to professional-looking working drawings.

The final chapter, "Installing Your Landscape," is filled with the tricks of the trade: from clearing and grading the site, to installing drainage and irrigation systems, to planting and maintaining the last annual.

Spend some time leisurely reading and looking through this book, and you will be well on your way to developing a complete landscape plan. Take your time; avoid making decisions just to complete the project quickly. In the long run, the results will be much more satisfying if you take the time necessary to envision exactly what you want.

Once you have a general concept in mind, don't expect to arrive at all the detailed decisions at once. Living with an unfinished landscape may be difficult at first. As you involve yourself in the landscaping process, you may find that it is more satisfying to develop slowly the perfect landscape than it is bothersome to have some bare earth for a while.

A LANDSCAPE OVERVIEW

The following are some basic concepts of landscaping to consider first, before beginning to develop a landscape plan. An understanding of these essential principles will help place all the other elements of this book in their proper perspective.

Public and Private Spaces

Land set aside and designed for the public has a different personality than land intended only for private use. Many privately maintained landscapes are, however, partly or entirely visible to the public. Just as in *Hamlet* Polonius says, "The apparel oft proclaims the man," so do the public aspects of your landscape reflect an image of you.

Decide which aspects of your landscape you regard as public and which ones you regard as private. In some countries, the entire residential environment is considered private; even friends are rarely asked to visit there. In the United States, homes are often used to entertain. Work out a division of public and private spaces that appeals to you. You may want the entire garden to be on display, or you may want some degree of separation from onlookers on the street. Most landscapes arrive at a compromise between these two points of view, devoting some space to public and some to private use. By making this distinction a conscious one, you will increase the likelihood of attaining just what you want.

Openly visible parts of the landscape can usually be converted into private or semiprivate spaces. You may need to build a fence, screen the garden from outside view with carefully chosen shrubs, or perhaps plant some trees to block out a neighboring building. If you are mainly concerned with the way the

house looks from the street and the impression it makes on people coming to the door, plan the garden accordingly.

The Borrowed Landscape

Although it is helpful to make the distinction between public and private land, you can also look at your landscape as actually extending beyond the limits of your property. In a sense, whatever you choose to notice becomes a part of your landscape. Your experience can be as limited or expansive as you choose to make it.

The principle of borrowed landscape can be applied to the street you live on and the neighbors' yards. Use the vistas and vegetation that happen to lie outside of your yard. Regardless

Above: A public front garden can give pleasure to both the homeowner and passersby.
Below: A handsome stone wall, some trees, and a gate create privacy while presenting an attractive scene to the outside world.

of the size of the plot, it can be expanded by incorporating views of the neighboring terrain. By opening the view, distant trees or mountains can be included in the landscape.

Perhaps you can work with your neighbor to plant trees and shrubs that hide the property line and make the two gardens appear as one. By visually merging two yards, a much more usable and pleasing space than either of the individual sites can be created. And some privacy can be maintained by screening certain areas.

In Japan the borrowed landscape is a long-practiced tradition. Low, mounding shrubs conceal property limits, but do not destroy the ability to enjoy the surroundings at large. A quarter-acre lot can be made to look much larger by cleverly locating the house, providing view spaces, and camouflaging the property boundaries with plantings. Unless surrounding views are unattractive, make use of them where possible. Don't plant a straight line of trees along the deed line. By doing so, you make the statement that nothing beyond your garden matters and that you want to block out any other view.

Neighborhood Landscaping

What you do within the confines of your yard makes an impression elsewhere. The trees you plant will be seen from afar as they grow, and flowers and shrubs will be appreciated by passersby. The attention you pay to the streetscape will eventually have an impact on the atmosphere of your own place. Plant the parking strips, if there are any, and consider planting street trees that will correspond with plantings in your garden. The more interest you take in the space surrounding your home, the more you will, in effect, own it.

Apartment dwellers can borrow the landscape in another way: by assuming responsibility for neglected public areas. For example, street trees could be watered, bulbs could be planted along the roadside for people in cars or busses to appreciate, and abandoned patches of greenery could be tended.

Neighborhood landscaping can include participating in antilittering efforts and in helping to control tree diseases and pests by spraying and pruning your own plants. As you take care of the larger landscape and show respect for it, neighbors may be inspired to do

the same. The result will be a greatly improved landscape for everyone to enjoy.

Taking Advantage of What You Have

Often, although a plan may be well intentioned, a landscape simply does not fit into the character of the neighborhood. It may fail to take advantage of the unique qualities of the site, following a plan that could have been used just as well in many other locations. On the other hand, just because a landscape is unique does not mean it will be pleasing.

Except in new subdivisions where the sites may be graded but unplanted, some kind of landscaping, however limited, usually exists. Whatever this older landscape is—a well-developed planting, a wild country spot with native trees, an apartment courtyard—make changes fit into the whole.

Make the most of what you have to work with. If you live in a condominium and a 10-by 20-foot patch of ground is the only space in which to landscape, consider the unique advantages of your situation. Your garden can be like a jewel box. Although you won't have room for large trees, you can certainly grow small ones in tubs, train vines onto an overhead canopy, or add the special atmosphere of

This tiny patio garden seems much larger than it is by borrowing the dramatic surrounding scenery.

Limited space need not limit garden aspirations. A small space can present a pleasant challenge for the urban gardener.

ing changes that complement existing architectural and natural surroundings. It also involves appreciating and incorporating the unique qualities of the area.

Before non-native plantings and other changes were brought about by housing developments, the character of an area had a special flavor. It may have been a dense, hardwood forest with craggy outcroppings, as Manhattan was until after the sixteenth century. Perhaps it was an open, grassy field, sparsely peppered with giant oak trees. Respect the genius of the place in creating gardens and landscapes. The genius is that special quality characteristic of the natural setting, unaltered by human hands. This respect demonstrates an attentiveness to and feeling for what is natural. But even if the neighborhood doesn't resemble the wild landscape that once existed there, the character or genius that has taken its place must also be respected.

To discover more about the native character of the property, drive out beyond populated areas to observe undeveloped nature. Is it flat, rolling, or steep? Is it forested or open? Observing the quality of this native land can serve you in two ways. First, it is a sure indication of what grows well in your area. Planting your landscape with native plants will not only blend them with the surroundings, it will reduce landscape maintenance. You actually work against nature when you use plants that do not grow well in the region.

Second, by following the natural landscape trends of the area, your individual landscape will fit into the environment and not look out of place. Your landscape will be a personalized extension of all that nature offers in that locality.

A native garden landscape could be designed by using only indigenous plants. Some gardeners feel that these are the most beautiful landscapes of all. Midwestern landscape architect Jens Jensen has stated that "To me no plant is more refined than that which belongs. There is no comparison between native plants and those imported from foreign shores which are and should always remain novelties .... Every plant has its features and must be placed in its proper surroundings so as to bring out its full beauty. Therein lies the art of landscaping."

a mountain stream with the aid of a simple Japanese splash-box. A limited amount of space needn't hamper your ability to design a charming outdoor area that improves the mood of your home.

Or you may own a big place in the country that needs landscaping. Consider the possibilities of creating areas that have an intimate quality, modifying the tree cover, siting auxiliary buildings, and establishing new roads, paths, and routes through the site.

Most outdoor environments fall somewhere in between the two extremes. A house will almost certainly have some sort of existing landscape that will need to be assessed in order to use it wisely, without wasting its existing qualities or potential.

Respecting the Genius of the Place

You will appreciate and enjoy nature more if you are alert to its needs, and if you work to satisfy them in the design of the garden. Designing a landscape is not only the art of mak-

This sentiment may be a bit severe, particularly since native plants may be difficult to obtain and may not suit everyone's particular landscaping tastes. But using native plants becomes more feasible if you include plants that resemble native varieties. For example, in an area that has a Mediterranean climate, where the native plants are accustomed to a five-to-seven-month drought each year, planting tropical varieties that require considerable summer irrigation invites extra expense and trouble. If you do so knowingly, you won't be disappointed, but if you are unaware that certain plants are poorly suited to your garden, you will be in for unexpected problems. By choosing plants at the nursery or garden center that are similar to those in the wild, you can get your landscape off to a head start. Read further about your home landscape and its larger environment on pages 19 to 23.

The Changing Qualities of Nature
Once you begin to expand your sensibilities to include your entire environment, you will start noticing things you've never seen before. Once you start noticing them, your interest is likely to be aroused. An appreciation of some of the subtler qualities of nature will increase landscaping possibilities immeasurably.

Consider the daylily flower that lasts for only a moment in the life of the garden, the tobacco flower that wafts its sweet scent only at night, the unexpected cluster of mushrooms, the flock of visiting birds feeding on the cotoneaster, the new fall of golden oak leaves and acorns. These short-lived but special moments all contribute to the garden show. Without these ephemeral qualities, the landscape would be much less exciting.

The appreciation of subtlety in nature has reached a peak in Japan. Before guests arrive, the Japanese host may rake and clean the garden, then sprinkle freshly fallen leaves on the raked paths to re-create a natural look.

By specifically planning for some of these delightful but short-lived garden features, you can build in surprises that will make your landscape a more captivating place.

Hedges, a bench, and shade from surrounding trees combine to create an intimate space within a larger garden.

Landscape Style

The style that you choose for your garden landscape may reflect traditional concepts or it may be highly individual. Whatever the style, it will almost certainly give you more satisfaction if you begin now, in the early planning stages, to consider carefully what landscape style means.

After helping you develop a working definition of style, this chapter will assist you in considering how your tastes, practical needs, and the garden's surroundings might affect the style you select. This discussion will first explore the concept of formality and informality; next, style and the environment; and, finally, style as a reflection of individuality and personal taste.

A landscape with a consistent design style has a special kind of integrity and coherence. It is not simply a collection of unrelated features and ideas, but a unified whole with parts that work together to achieve an overall effect. A landscape designed with a specific style has a look, whereas landscapes without a coherent style often are visually confusing. A landscape without unity, for example, would be one where Japanese artifacts, such as a lantern, water dipper, and miniature bridge, have been placed in the midst of a cottage-style garden or adjacent to a Tudor home. However, if these same artifacts were set in a traditional Japanese garden—or even a simple garden without a specific style—they would be in harmony with their surroundings. An awareness of your garden's natural and man-made surroundings is essential to the development of a coherent landscape style.

A garden need not be modeled after a particular style in order to be coherent. Whether it's traditional, contemporary, or personal, the landscape style should never be at odds with its surroundings.

This southwestern landscape reflects its surroundings, while presenting a design all its own.

A landscape with consistent style has a special sense of integrity and coherence.

It is important for you to consider the relationship between style and fashion. Fashions change with the prevailing tastes of the time and place, with one fashion replacing another. Certain fashions are repeated again and again in certain regions because of how well they suit the existing conditions. By contrast, style is consciously developed and is harmonious with both the place and the person. Style reflects the choices and personality of the designer. A garden that suits one region or even one person will very likely be ill-suited to other regions or other people—a Connecticut garden, for example, in an arid, severe terrain. As you consider what your style is and how you would like to incorporate it into your design, consider what design elements best suit you and the landscape surrounding your garden—and not simply what fashion happens to be currently popular.

FORMALITY AND INFORMALITY

When thinking of style in the garden, you may think in terms of formal versus informal. One basic reason for making a garden is to create some degree of organization (or formality) out of the natural (informal) setting. At one extreme, absolute formality in a landscape is represented by the reduction of all natural elements to geometric shapes. At this extreme, the landscape eliminates plants, as even carefully pruned topiary has subtle irregularities. The other extreme, absolute informality, is complete naturalness, as is found in the untouched wilderness, where no hand has modified natural forms or imposed any sort of human order.

It is more reasonable to think of a style that falls somewhere between these two extremes and that combines elements of each.

There is no right or wrong balance between formality and informality. In keeping with the idea of coherence in the garden, the successful choice is the one that suits both the setting and your tastes.

Breaking the formal-informal concept down into pairs of more specific opposing elements—symmetry versus asymmetry, structure versus lack of structure—can help to pinpoint the degree of formality most appropriate for the landscape.

Symmetry and Asymmetry

Many people think of formality in the landscape in terms of symmetry. Symmetry is fundamental to many human concepts and creations, from the practical to the aesthetic.

Symmetry has characterized many landscape styles throughout history. Ancient Egyptians made gardens with symmetry based on the straight lines and square angles of agriculture. This symmetrical style was refined in Persia and the Middle East, and came to Spain and Italy with the Moors. As it spread, symmetry was adapted to the unique needs and tastes of each culture. In later centuries, expansive gardens such as those at Versailles—and more modest ones in European and British homes—embodied the same idea, expressing symmetry in many forms, from simple geometry to elaborate intricacy.

Although some traditional Japanese gardens are completely or partially symmetrical, the more subtle concept of asymmetry characterizes most gardens in Japan. At first glance their features seem to be arranged randomly, but in fact they are carefully positioned to achieve an asymmetry that appears balanced from all points of viewing. In Japanese landscaping, the visual impact of a landscape feature is determined by both its physical mass and its visual weight. For example, a brightly colored or visually striking object may have as much, or more, visual impact as a heavy stone or structure.

Symmetrical balance is obvious; asymmetrical balance, though no less real, is less readily perceived. A landscape in which asymmetrical balance is used may appear to be natural and informal, whereas it is just as formal—in the sense of being organized and

Left: Symmetry and clipped, simple plantings characterize the formal garden. Right: Visual weight can be as important as actual weight in achieving a balanced effect. The brightly blooming azalea is visually striking and complements the heavy stone lantern.

Right: The angular, symmetrical lines of this garden are tempered by the loose, unclipped herb and vegetable garden they contain.
Below: A pleasant meadowlike effect is created by the choice and placement of harmonious plantings.

balanced—as a landscape with symmetry. Because it is balanced, its apparently random, natural look feels extraordinarily stable, as though it had existed that way for many years.

Informal, highly naturalistic gardens, whose design owes nothing to either symmetrical or asymmetrical principles, have existed since the beginning of garden building. For the most part, these were attempts to re-create a natural paradise. If a very informal look is desired, asymmetrical balance need not necessarily be a concern. A pleasant, natural effect can be achieved by choosing and arranging garden elements to suggest a natural landscape. Careful observation of settings in nature that appeal to you will provide an excellent guide to the selection and placement of plants, rocks, and other elements. You may also want to impose a touch of symmetry to provide a visual focus within a natural setting—for instance, a rustic, vine-covered arbor set in a meadow and woodland landscape. The juxtaposition of the nonsymmetrical natural landscape and the symmetrical man-made arbor adds interest and appeal to the garden.

Structure and Lack of Structure

A structured garden is one in which the design is obvious. For example, almost all buildings or constructed features—decks, paths, patios—will give a strong sense of structure. Most gardens in the formal style clearly show their design. Heavily pruned plants, such as boxwood shrubs that have been carefully shaped into topiary, will give the same impression. A curving brick walkway obviously reveals the human hand in the garden as well, yet its clear-cut structure is softened by curves that temper the overall effect.

An entire garden—or any part of it—can be unstructured. A garden can combine elements that have been placed there by nature and by hand. Instead of straight lines and angles, circles or gentle curves are employed. An open, arching shrub is used in place of a sheared one. Even architectural elements can be softened in their structured appearance through weathering. Raw wood, for example, will darken or turn gray, assuming a softness that unites it with nature. Bricks in a walkway begin to wear slightly, replacing the bright colors of new brick with more earthy tones. As you think about what sort of landscape style will work best, consider both how much structure to include and how that structure will change with time.

STYLE AND THE ENVIRONMENT

In order to determine exactly how formal a landscape style should be—where and to what extent symmetry and asymmetry will be used, and the structure or lack of structure—you must first take a long, thoughtful look at the place and its context.

The site of your future garden, a particular piece of ground adjacent to your house, must accommodate the architectural style of that house. It lies close to, and must coexist with, other home landscapes in your neighborhood. And it is inescapably part of a geographic region, whose climate, topography, native vegetation, and perhaps traditional garden styles you should examine before committing yourself to a particular style.

Architecture of Your House

To be effective, the style of your landscape must be compatible with the architectural style of your house. If the house is designed in a particular period style—Spanish-American colonial or English Tudor, for instance—one possibility is to design a landscape that reflects the same period. Researching the authentic landscape style for your house can be a fascinating, gratifying undertaking. But

Look to the surrounding landscape for inspiration. Native trees and flowers incorporated in this city garden give a natural feeling of open space.

Matching the style of the garden with the architecture of the house is an important part of landscape design and can increase the appeal of both.

strict adherence to a period style is limiting and, in some cases, labor-intensive—for example, shearing hedges, shaping topiary, and maintaining borders or beds, in addition to the preliminary research. It could also be impractical; for example, materials might be unavailable or too costly, the terrain and space might be unsuitable, or traditional plants might be horticulturally inappropriate.

A more workable and at least as aesthetically pleasing solution is to use a style that simply is compatible with the house. If the house is symmetrical and the yard is level or nearly so, symmetry and a high degree of structure in the garden are appropriate. Or you can make more extensive use of symmetry near the house and, if the property is spacious, create transitional areas toward a more relaxed style farther away from the house. An older house without pronounced symmetry or the strong suggestion of a period might be surrounded by a garden of an informal style. If the house is modern and its lines are simple and clean, rather than heavily ornamented or evocative of a period style, almost any style,

including Japanese, could be adapted to suit your needs.

The best approach is to study the atmosphere that the house creates in its setting. If that atmosphere is appealing, decide how the style of the garden might enhance it. If the atmosphere is not appealing, consider what style might best neutralize or mask the deficiencies of the house.

Be realistic about the topography of your property and its size relative to the size of the house. Uneven terrain, where alterations are impractical or undesirable, lends itself to simple, asymmetrical designs. An unusually spacious lot invites bold effects or a division of the property into different areas, whose styles may vary to some extent, as long as they are screened from each other and do not clash.

Surrounding Gardens

Does a discernible style prevail in your neighborhood? Walk and look, especially if you are new to the area. Notice whether there is any sort of unity, if only in plant selections, in the overall neighborhood landscape. If so, what

Right: This garden blends well with, and borrows from, the natural surroundings, yet has a style all its own.
Below: Working together, these neighbors have created a harmonious community landscape.

can be done to unify your garden with those surrounding it? If, on the other hand, your neighborhood landscape is a patchwork of styles, what can you do with your property to help minimize that effect—or at least to avoid intensifying it?

In some neighborhoods in parts of the southeastern United States, a satisfying style is achieved by minimizing boundary markers—fences, walls, hedges, and screens between front gardens—and leaving or planting the indigenous longleaf pines. This creates, in effect, an unbroken sweep of lawn and airy pines that can be underplanted with azaleas, camellias, and dogwoods, occasionally punctuated with southern magnolias. It is a style with strong seasonal interest, relation to the natural surroundings, sense of regional tradition, and perfect horticultural appropriateness. The unity and continuity make the sense of neighborhood more complete.

Regional Environment

In deciding on an appropriate landscape style, you need to consider your garden in the broad

context of the region. It's imperative to study natural characteristics of the area where you live, especially topography, weather, and native vegetation, if your style is to have integrity and practicality. If you live in a region with a traditional landscaping style—which developed because of its appropriateness to the natural characteristics of the region—you may decide to adopt or borrow from it.

Looking to nature   Even if you're a city dweller with a tiny plot of land deep in a man-made canyon of brick, steel, and concrete, you must at least consider climate before settling on an appropriate garden style. If you live in suburb, town, or open country, the relation of your outdoor space to its natural context necessitates looking at the native vegetation and prevailing topography of the region (particularly the topography in which, or within view of which, your property lies).

An English-style garden may look out of place and function poorly in southern California. On the other hand, the sort of southeastern

landscape style described on page 21 works well in parts of the Southeast, largely because it uses plantings native to the region.

In a southwestern garden, the colors and contours of nearby mountains and expanses of flat land might influence style as strongly as aridity and extreme summer heat do.

The style of a northern garden might be determined to an extent by the need to trap and hold solar heat in one or more protected, south-facing areas. Native trees and shrubs would make a link with the natural environment and withstand the rigors of winter.

Northern California's Mediterranean climate influences plant selection in many environmentally appropriate gardens there, and the area's Mediterranean light invites styles that take advantage of the vividness of color.

Looking to tradition   Many regions of the United States have traditional styles. Some were established early and have strong ethnic flavor. For instance, in California and the Southwest the Spanish-American courtyard

Roberto Burle-Marx's abstract landscapes use a variety of exotic plant materials combined with swirling forms and undulating curves.

garden provides shelter from parching winds, some shade from blazing sunlight, touches of color, and the luxury of splashing water. (Read more about this style on page 27.)

Other styles considered to be traditional are more recent in origin. For example, the northern California style began to emerge before the midtwentieth century, as the population of the area swelled and residential development boomed. Landscape architect Thomas Church, largely responsible for this style, recognized the need for gardens that reflect the pleasures of almost year-round indoor-outdoor living in a gentle climate. He also believed in using widely available and relatively low-cost materials such as concrete, asphalt, gravel, and wood to create modern, low-maintenance terraces—and other paved surfaces—which were descendants of the Spanish-American indoor-outdoor gardens. By mixing geometric and free forms, Church created gardens that bore his unmistakable stamp, yet always suited their sites and the individual needs and tastes of his clients.

STYLE AND YOU

Just as Thomas Church adjusted his style to each client, you should choose or develop a style that suits you and your family exactly. The word *style* derives from the Latin word *stilus*, which relates, among other things, to the concept of the individual style expressed in a person's handwriting. Landscape style, at its best and most interesting, is to some degree as personal as handwriting.

A logical, practical first step toward developing a personal style is to identify what needs the landscape should satisfy. See the Design Checklist on page 70 for ways to determine those needs.

Your needs will help to determine the design itself—the landscape's functions, and its features and their arrangement—and also its style. If you're an avid gardener and collector of plants, maintaining unity and a necessary degree of order will be challenging and the resulting style will perhaps be lush, highly textured, and colorful. Or, if an important need is simply to create a low-maintenance landscape, your garden might have many structures, including paved or decked areas, and few plantings, with a resulting style that is spare, clean, and simple.

You might take inspiration from ways in which well-known garden designers have let personal interests help to define their styles. For instance, Gertrude Jekyll, a celebrated English garden designer, was first of all a painter concerned with color and the myriad possibilities in color schemes, so her landscape style incorporated subtle, exquisite uses of color. Brazilian landscape designer Roberto Burle-Marx, also a painter, has developed a style characterized by the bold patterns of modern abstract painting, using swirls, undulating curves, and a broad palette of striking and unusual plants. Thomas Church's gardens are designed to take greatest advantage of the landscape, connecting outside and inside living for maximum enjoyment and benefit of the homeowner.

Remember above all: Instead of setting out to create a style that you suppose will please others, first try to please yourself. Even if you settle on a traditional style, you will probably enjoy your landscape more if it has personal touches.

Left: This wild landscape in the Southeast was created by transplanting native trees, shrubs, and wildflowers from the surrounding countryside.
Right: The wild landscape may exist anywhere. Here, the natural vegetation of the desert has barely been altered to create a garden that unites the house and desert.

A SAMPLER OF LANDSCAPE STYLES

Of the numerous traditional landscape styles used today in the United States, several popular ones representing a broad spectrum of concepts are discussed on the following pages. Study each style that appeals to you, and determine what it is that attracts you. If some styles have little appeal, try to understand what makes them less attractive than others; perhaps some of their subtler elements might still be useful to you.

As you look at other landscapes for ideas, consider the reasonable limits of the native landscape and use restraint and care in combining a number of styles. Yet, you may find ideas in one or several of the featured landscapes that will inspire and move you closer to understanding exactly which style is right for you and your garden site.

The Wild Garden

Often termed "the woodland garden" in areas of natural woodland, the wild garden may suggest, if not actually attempt to replicate, the native countryside, or some facet of it—whether meadow, sandy desert, rocky and sparsely vegetated mountains, grassy plain, chaparral, or rugged or smooth coastline. Simplification of the natural terrain is usually the key to successful expression of such a style. For example, the complexities of an actual woodland, which would likely create a hopelessly crowded, disunified effect in the confines of a typical yard area, might be gracefully reduced to two or three mossy native stones, a planting of three appropriate trees, perhaps of the same species, a clump of ferns, one native ground cover, several native shrubs, and, at the drip line of the trees, apparently natural clumps of spring bulbs,

either native to the area or wild, and harmonious with the native landscape. Whichever wild landscape you decide to design, be sure it is a simple and accurate re-creation of the natural landscape in your area that it is intended to represent.

The Formal Garden

The rigidity of the formal landscape, with its clipped plantings and strict use of geometric forms superimposed on the landscape, may strike contemporary gardeners as a bit too severe for today's way of living. Even so, the formal style has enjoyed renewed interest in recent years, in part due to the efforts of landscape designers. It has broadened in definition as more gardeners adapt the basic concepts to their own needs and settings.

The formal, ordered landscape developed from the need to achieve the most from limited space within the walls of a manor house, castle, or monastery. Planting in tight, geometric beds was as much a matter of efficiency and convenience as it was a conscious stylistic choice.

Over time, the formal style became more defined and consistent and was translated to much larger and more diverse settings, but the essential characteristics remained. Today, the formal style may be seen in sites ranging from the small, urban garden to the open, unfenced expanse of the suburban yard with a variety of plants used.

The Knot Garden

This ancient style is characterized by an appealing tension between the symmetry of the overall design and the looseness of the plantings. Some "knots," however, are rigidly designed and maintained, with carefully clipped, diminutive evergreen hedges or intricately patterned beds of flowers. A popular use of the knot-garden style today is for the growing of herbs. Scents, many shades of green, and variety in texture lend particular charm and interest to this loose form of the knot.

A knot may be incorporated into a larger garden as a "room," sunken below the level of adjacent areas or separated by walls or hedges. This is often the ideal style for a small, flat urban plot that is viewed from windows or a terrace above.

Left: Formal gardens are characterized by clipped plantings and strict use of geometric forms superimposed on the landscape. Sculptures or other man-made structures can be placed to draw the viewer's eye along a particular line of sight.
Right: The knot garden is another variety of the formal style. Intricate patterns are created with a variety of clipped shrubs, sculptures, and lawn.

Above: This house, with its rustic exterior and cottage-style garden has a country feeling, although it is in an urban setting. Above right: A stone lantern, slab bridge, and pond create a Japanese effect in one small corner of this garden. Below right: This carefully tended Japanese garden resembles a painting when viewed from the house. Rich in varied textures and forms, the landscape is a microcosm of nature.

The Cottage Garden

Humble in its origins, the cottage garden of England and early New England is small, unstructured, crowded, and colorful. An early settler in America described the sweet simplicity of his cottage garden as "gay with a variety of flowers, including the fair white lily and sweet fragrant rose." Typical in the New World version was a picket fence, covered with vines and climbing vegetables, built to keep out the livestock.

Historically the cottage garden has had its practical uses: furnishing food, scent makers, dyes, cleansing agents, insecticides, medicinal herbs, lotions, and cosmetics. Because the cottage garden lends itself to a small space, its looseness calls for little, if any, pruning and shaping. Its unrestrained variety appeals to plant collectors, and its colorful beauty endures and changes throughout the growing season. Something of the effect of an expansive English herbaceous border can be realized in a small space. Today the style has returned to favor. An authentic example of the cottage-style garden may be seen at the Whipple House in Ipswich, Massachusetts.

The Japanese Garden

The Japanese have developed a number of distinctive garden styles, but to the Western eye some generalized aspects and particular features characterize this group of styles and, with great restraint, can often be combined in one garden. The purpose of a Japanese garden is to provide a quiet sanctuary in which the visitor can forget worldly cares and contemplate nature. The garden is enclosed. Nature is simplified, so that its essence is revealed. The garden's apparent randomness, upon close inspection, proves to be a subtle and sophisticated asymmetrical formality.

Plantings are simple, colors are extremely limited (often only shades of green), artifacts are few and simple, and structures are weathered and full-size rather than miniature. Water, if only in a rustic stone basin, reflects the sky and completes the picture of tranquility.

The Courtyard Garden

The gardens of old Mexico, California, and the Southwest, descendants of the most ancient of gardens, lay usually within courtyards, shut off from the harsh, arid landscape beyond. They were oases that could, in many cases, be looked into and entered from nearly every room in the house. Water splashing in a centrally placed fountain provided a sense of lush coolness and repose. Fragrance and color pervaded both the garden and adjoining rooms of the house.

Modern versions do not have to be used in conjunction with Spanish architecture. Any enclosed patio or atrium with a fountain and a symmetrical layout can create much the same effect without suggesting a historical period or a region. Colorful tile or paving surfaces and lush, tropical plants will help create a courtyard effect.

Above left: Container plants and ivy turn this small courtyard into a lush oasis.
Above right: This garden was designed to blend with the surrounding region.
Center left: Japanese bonsai provide a pleasant contrast to the traditional Spanish style of the house.
Center right: Lichen-covered rocks and arid-climate plantings create a natural style.
Lower left: A small, condominium entryway has been transformed into an elegant showpiece.

The Elements Of Design

No matter what garden style appeals to you, a successful landscape requires the use of basic design principles. Knowing these principles and how to use them well will enable you to create the look and feeling you want.

Take a moment to think of a favorite garden landscape, either real or imagined. What stands out after studying this landscape? What components of the setting make it distinctive?

The trees, shrubs, vines, flowers, and other plants are probably noticeable. Other obvious elements are the physical confines of the site, such as the fences and hedges that define the property line, and the house and the outdoor living areas, such as patios, walkways, decks, and other structures.

Next, pretend you are viewing this landscape from a hot-air balloon high off the ground. Notice how the garden relates to neighboring gardens and to the surrounding area in general. When the landscape is viewed from this height, does the garden appear to have an overall design? Do the textures, colors, sizes, and forms of the plants create a distinctive, balanced whole? Are the outdoor living areas clearly defined? Is the garden designed for people, with places for the activities that will make it come alive? Does a single style predominate? If so, does it complement the house, and does it fit in well with the surroundings? The degree to which each element is considered in creating the garden plan will determine how effective and attractive the final landscape will be.

A successful design combines many elements—both natural and man-made—and is in keeping with its setting.

Left: The graceful, upward-reaching shapes of the tree trunks, mirrored by the ferns and shrubs and dramatically back-lit by the sun, are stunning examples of the natural forces at work in the landscape. Right: When designing a landscape, imagine what it will look like from high in the air. When viewed from above, the design becomes apparent.

Designing a landscape is not simply an ordered process of working with a known set of elements. As with any creative project, the whole of a successful landscape more than equals the sum of its parts. A memorable landscape—whether natural or man-made—makes an impression on the viewer on many different levels, some of which are quite subtle. This subtle quality is sometimes referred to as the force of a landscape.

This special force can be present in designed landscapes as well as natural landscapes. To create force, the designer must be sensitive to how all the elements in a landscape are combined. Take another look at the photographs in the second chapter. In addition to showing a distinct landscape style,

each example also possesses a force that unifies everything. If there is magic in design, this is it: the ability to perceive and re-create a balance among the forces in nature.

When this force is missing, the result is often visually ambiguous—the product of uncertain intentions. In a landscape that lacks intent, the materials and space fail to achieve a balance, with displeasing effects.

THE DESIGN PROCESS

Designing and creating a landscape can be as much a source of pleasure as enjoying the final product. The process of design, which involves the evolution of your thoughts about your garden and the possibilities for modifying it, begins by discovering new ways of understanding the existing landscape. Three steps help lead to this understanding: *survey*, *evaluation*, and *synthesis*.

Survey   All the basic information that relates to your garden should be included in the survey. Basic conditions—topography and existing plants, buildings, walkways, and other permanent features—are surveyed to discover what materials are available.

Evaluation   The second step involves analyzing the results of the survey to decide what is most important to change and what can be postponed. The avid gardener or professional landscaper never really finishes evaluating a garden. As new landscaping ideas emerge or as needs and tastes change, the landscape will also undergo transformation. Reevaluating a garden is a constant but pleasant task.

Synthesis Assessing the information gathered during the survey will help draw together and form ideas about the garden. By examining the features of the landscape and the priorities for changing it, you can begin to create a design.

First, familiarize yourself with the following design elements and apply them to the present landscape, element by element. This process will lead to new ways to view the landscape and will offer a solid basis for making design decisions.

THE ELEMENTS OF PERSPECTIVE

The use of perspective is essential in any landscape design. Careful planning and thoughtful selection of plants and materials can cleverly and subtly influence the viewer's perception of a garden landscape.

View Positions

These are the particular spots from which the landscape is customarily seen. One view position might be from a window at the kitchen table, where you sit each morning and evening. Others might be a patio looking west and south, and the front walkway leading to the door. Most landscapes have many view positions. To make them easier to identify, the vantage points of these positions can be grouped into three categories.

The view from above As a child, you may have spied out of a second-story window onto the garden below and felt in command of the situation, able to see things that eluded the people on the ground. The view from a tree house or a hillside deck can provide a similar sense of exhilaration. This perspective also creates a feeling of space, detachment, and, perhaps, insecurity.

The level view The world is most often viewed from a level position. When experienced on the horizontal plane, the scale of the objects in the landscape and the shadows they

View Positions

Above: The addition of a multilevel deck provides several viewing points, greatly enhancing the visual appeal of the garden. The existing tree was left intact to provide natural shelter and shade to the deck.
Left: The view from above shows the shape and form of the garden and also gives the viewer a sense of power.

cast are the most familiar. The level view is secure, less exciting than others, but it is the most common one in garden landscapes.

The view from below   This position exists, for example, when a house is situated in a canyon or a patio is built on the lower slope of a hill. Viewing the landscape from below may provide feelings of security or enclosure, or it may feel oppressive. Being aware of the potentials and drawbacks of this position will help you to decide if it has a place in your garden landscape.

Foreground, Midground, and Background

When you stand in one place in a garden, what are the relationships among the things that you see? Generally, objects in the foreground are more detailed than those in the background. The midground has greater clarity than the background, but not as much as the foreground. Notice how these perspectives change from different locations in the landscape. Try identifying these three primary fields of view from different positions. Determine why you prefer particular perspectives and consider how they may be incorporated and strengthened in the design of the garden.

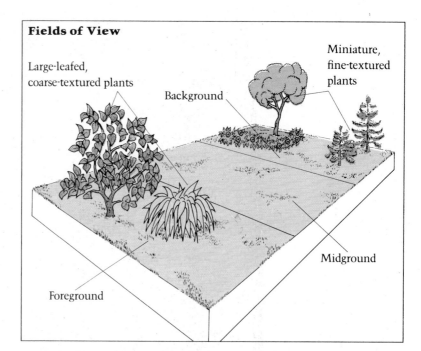

Fields of View

Large-leafed, coarse-textured plants

Miniature, fine-textured plants

Background

Midground

Foreground

Right: The tea house and weeping cypress next to it appear to be much farther away from the viewer than they actually are. In fact, the tea house is only 6 feet tall, and the cypress is a dwarf form of a much larger variety. The landscape creates the illusion of a deeper lot.
Opposite left: The view from below can contribute to a feeling of security and enclosure.
Opposite right: Different textures placed in the fore-, mid-, and background of the landscape increase contrast and make this garden more pleasant and visually appealing.

Forcing Perspective

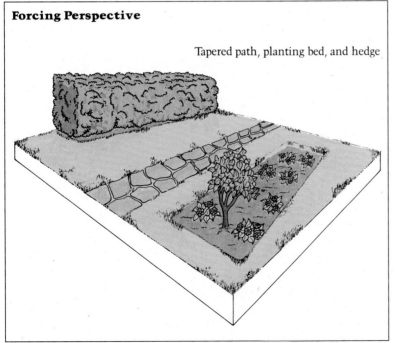

Tapered path, planting bed, and hedge

Forcing Perspective

The way a garden is viewed may be manipulated by working with the various fields of vision. Forcing perspective can cause the viewer to perceive objects as being farther away than they actually are. This may be achieved by using exaggerated contrasts in size and texture: arranging small, finely textured plantings in the background and large, coarsely textured ones in the foreground. Because the finer-textured plantings appear more distant than the coarse ones, the viewer has an impression of greater depth than actually exists in the garden.

If a yard is wide and shallow, it can be made to appear deeper by tapering planting beds or walkways so that they are narrower toward the rear of the garden. If beds or walkways are widened toward the rear of the garden, the space will look shallower.

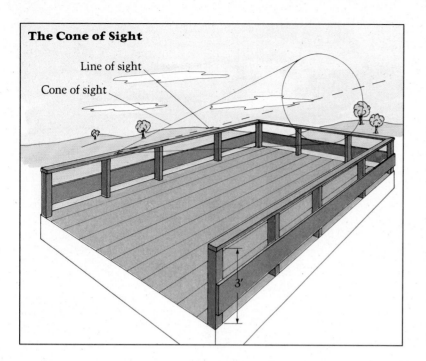

The Cone of Sight

Line of sight

Cone of sight

3'

plete the height requirement. See the discussion of enclosure on pages 39 and 40.

Line of Sight

In about the middle of the cone of sight, the area of the horizontal view (seen from a standing or sitting position) between 3 and 6 feet above ground level is called the line of sight. This important zone represents the viewer's primary area of vision. Obstructions to the view along the line of sight can be very discomforting, particularly if the view extends both below and above, as from a high deck. If the line of sight must be blocked for more than a few inches, consider obstructing it completely with a wall or fence.

Axes in the Landscape

Standing or sitting in a garden or on a patio, a viewer tends to look at certain objects or in certain directions, focusing on what attracts attention within the line of sight. In a well-conceived landscape design, objects with special visual appeal and prominence are placed intentionally within the viewer's line of sight. Careful location of plants and structures also creates an axis that directs the viewer's attention. In the absence of an axis, what falls within the line of sight will be random and may be unappealing. In designing a garden, consider creating axes to direct the viewer's line of sight to the most attractive features of the landscape.

In formal landscapes, axes are used to direct and emphasize lines of sight, and because of their strong, geometric simplicity, they are an integral part of the formal style. The intentionally linear design of the formal garden is the reason garden sculpture or specimen plants are placed at the end of axis lines, where the eye will invariably come to rest.

In an informal garden, axis lines are more subtle, created by suggested lines of sight. Although they are not obvious, they are still important. Implied axes may be formed by pavement patterns, night lighting, the shape of a clearing through the woods, lawn areas, and many other elements that are either contrived or natural. Suggested axes can be quite powerful, particularly if they are emphasized and remain uninterrupted. A specimen shrub, for example, can be pruned to open up a distant view. Strategic placement of containers

The Cone of Sight

At any given time, the viewer in an outdoor space sees a roughly cone-shaped area about 8 feet in diameter, called the cone of sight (see illustration above). When the view within this zone is interrupted—by a deck railing, a fence, or another physical barrier—a feeling of enclosure is created. If the view is blocked by large objects or walls, the sense of enclosure may seem severe and oppressive.

It may be desirable to have both an enclosure and a distant view; for example, a deck on a steep hillside that requires a railing for security but which does not obstruct the view. A railing no more than 3½ feet tall will lend a secure feeling but not block the viewer's cone of sight. Remember, if the deck is higher than 3 feet above ground, the federal Uniform Building Code requires that the railing be at least 36 inches high and not contain an opening greater than 9 inches. (This code, which is intended to prevent children from falling off high decks, may vary from state to state, or from county to county.)

To fulfill safety requirements without producing the feeling of being caged in, make only part of the vertical enclosure solid. As one way to do this, leave about 3 inches along the bottom open in order to sweep away leaves and other debris, followed by a solid panel, 2 feet wide, that runs the entire perimeter of the deck. Above that, a simple capping of 2 by 6 lumber, leaving a 9-inch opening, will com-

Landscape Axis

The eye of the viewer is drawn along the curved line of the path and away from an unattractive view of a neighboring garage. The tree and shrub to the left also screen the view.

Line of sight

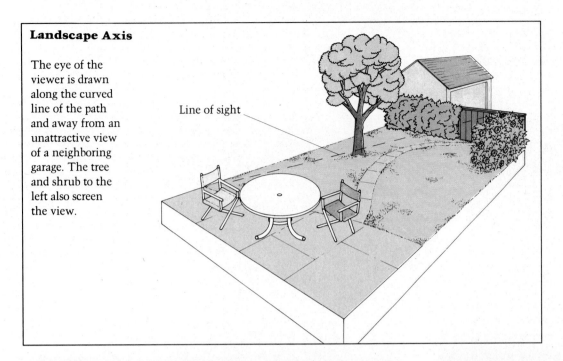

of plants helps to move the eye along an entryway and from another direction provides focus for a flower bed. In studying a site, look for the naturally occurring axes and for ways to strengthen them.

Mystery

In a garden, mystery is pleasing as long as a solution is suggested. It is never pleasant to enter a maze when an escape route is not evident. Baffled walls lend mystery to any landscape, because they keep the viewer from seeing exactly what lies beyond them. A baffle can consist of a series of vertical panels, 6 or 8 inches wide and about 6 feet high. Viewers walking past the louvers see just a hint of what is on the other side, as it flickers past like an old-time movie.

Another visual trick is to extend the ground plane out of sight around a solid object. An axis of the landscape may end where a lawn disappears beyond a mass of shrubs, so that the viewer wonders where the lawn actually terminates. The lawn may appear to extend for some distance, when it actually reaches only a few feet behind the shrubs. It is intriguing to look at because it can't be seen in its entirety. Paths in the garden and private sections of decks and patios can also take advantage of similar design tricks by disappearing from sight, perhaps to reappear later in another part of the garden.

Left: The viewer's eye is subtly drawn in two directions—toward the lantern and along the path—in this Japanese-style garden. The viewer is encouraged to stop and appreciate the scene, although the path forward is clearly marked.
Right: Overhanging boughs, vines, and massed plantings obscure the view, and lend an air of mystery about what lies ahead.

A wonderful sense of mystery pervades those traditional Japanese gardens designed according to the principle known as hide and reveal. Instead of being disclosed all at once from one vantage point, various features of a garden come into view in a sequence. A path disappearing beyond shrubbery, over a rise, or around the corner of a building draws the stroller along and encourages exploration. These visual mysteries and their subsequent solutions create a delightful rhythm that can be achieved in a garden even if its style is not Japanese.

Relative Size

Outdoor rooms are most successful when their size conforms to their intended use. For example, an intimate private patio should probably be about the size of an intimate indoor sitting room. A barbecue cooking and eating area intended for entertaining should be about the same size as a kitchen–dining room combination of comfortable dimensions inside the house.

If a style of entertaining calls for large interior rooms, the outdoor rooms should also be large. Be careful, however, because there's a tendency to make outdoor spaces much bigger than they need to be, which can lead to uncomfortably large areas lacking a feeling of enclosure.

The most desirable places to sit outdoors are like the backwaters of a stream, where eddies exist out of the way of fast-moving water. They provide a feeling of repose and a restful sense of apartness.

Try creating smaller spaces within a larger one by placing tubs of plants or groupings of furniture to simulate edges of space. The modification can be made more permanent by alternating paved areas with planting beds filled to a pleasing height. In a landscape that is being redone, look critically at the existing living spaces, and be daring. Make spaces smaller or larger, or move them to a different part of the yard.

Human Scale

General rules about space have so many exceptions that they are useful only as starting points. One such rule states that space is most comfortable when it has a relationship to the scale of the human form.

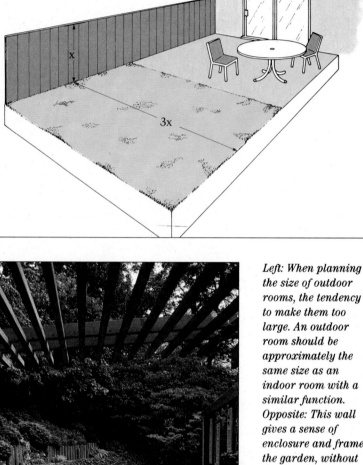

Human Scale

Left: When planning the size of outdoor rooms, the tendency is to make them too large. An outdoor room should be approximately the same size as an indoor room with a similar function. Opposite: This wall gives a sense of enclosure and frames the garden, without blocking the view to neighboring gardens.

An enclosed space takes on human scale when the wall height equals one half to one third of the width of the space. When walls are less than one fourth as high as the width, the area may not appear to be enclosed or to have any scale at all. When walls exceed one half the width of the space, the enclosure can seem oppressive.

A landscape can achieve relative human proportions whether the scale is large or small. A large garden with a view of mountains in the distance can be as human in scale as a small rock garden—if the view is open and expansive. However, if the garden is narrow and lined on both sides by tall trees, the distant mountains will appear too tall in proportion to the size of the lot.

Connections

A landscape is influenced not only by open space and enclosure, but also by the way viewers enter and pass from one area to another. In planning a landscape, keep in mind that easy flow between areas is central to enjoying a garden.

Consider the close connection between a tool shed and a vegetable garden, a vegetable garden and a kitchen, a barbecue area and a family room, a hot tub and a lanai or master bedroom. The overall pattern of connections in the landscape constitutes the garden's circulation: how a viewer enters and moves around and through the landscape, whether by paths, patios, boardwalks, stepping-stones, decks, or steps.

When outlining a landscape on paper, first visualize and sketch ways in which the areas in a yard can relate to each other. These sketches are part of the bubble plan stage of design (see page 71). At this point in the survey of a site, it is necessary to think only about the general character of the garden spaces and their uses. Various arrangements result in different circulation patterns. For example, the dining room can be opened up by adding French doors that provide access to the patio and outdoor cooking area. Making bubble plans allows you to see a previously unnoticed connection.

Circulation can sometimes be thought out in advance, but actual use is the best way to determine where connections should be placed. It is preferable to allow connections to develop, then add paths based on where the ground is most worn. The paths at one junior college were made in this way; after the first few months of student traffic, the most popular lines of travel became obvious.

The shortest route between two places is usually the best one, if utility is the primary consideration. A landscape that is designed

Connections

Patio, barbecue, hot tub, vegetable garden, tool shed, and areas of repose are connected by carefully planned routes.

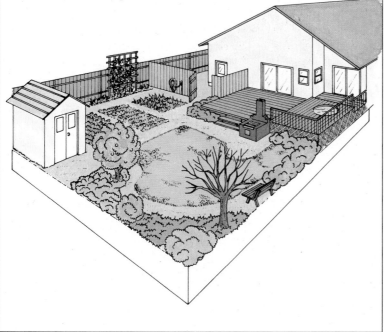

Style and placement of paths contribute to the overall effect of a garden. The owners of this garden chose a meandering, unpaved path that encourages strolling and provides points of interest along the way.

with aesthetics in mind may eliminate the most evident paths, however, and let paths wander by certain trees, around garden sculpture, or past revealing views.

Sequence

A residential landscape should contain a general indication of where a path leads—to the front door, garage, tool shed, and so forth. Excitement, even mystery, can be generated if the direction is handled in a less than straightforward manner. A path can head off at right angles to the front door before returning to its more obvious destination. Landscape architect Lockwood de Forest ordered the sequence of views from the entry driveway of a large estate by alternately revealing the house across sweeping lawns and concealing it behind masses of shrubs, occasionally showing off a specimen tree or rustic bench nestled in a hedgerow.

Sequence

The most direct route is not always the most desirable. Plan walkways to provide a sequence of visual experiences for the enjoyment of those using them.

Changes of scene can make the process of approaching the front door an adventure rich in sensory experiences. Each site has its own possibilities; try making a few bubble plans to discover sequences for your front yard.

THE ELEMENTS OF FORM

The presence of forms and their interrelationships play a fundamental role in the creation of a landscape. Forms fill the landscape—the round slope of a hillside, the crown of a mature oak, a marigold blossom, a redwood tree, an A-frame house, a topiary garden sculpture, an outline of a skyscraper, a lean-to shed, a drain inlet, a cliff face, the repetition of hill upon hill receding in the distance, the symmetry of a grove of trees.

A successful landscape contains forms that balance and complement each other. Too much height, too many curves, too many rectangles, or other excesses not only may be ugly, but also may make the viewer ill at ease.

Forms also need to relate well according to their size. A circular flower bed measuring 10 feet in diameter might work well next to a circular bed of 5 feet across because of the significant difference in size between the two. Two adjoining circles that are 10 and 8 feet across may be too similar in size to create a meaningful contrast.

In the same way, try to use angles repetitively, but avoid combining too many varying angles in a limited space, which will weaken a design considerably. Stay with angle families, such as 30, 60, and 90 degrees or 45, 90, 180, and 360 degrees. In using contrasting angles, try to tie them into right angles at some point in the design.

Reinforce two-dimensional forms, such as a circular lawn or a rectangular patio, with three-dimensional masses of shrubs and other solid forms. In a circular lawn, for example, make the walk around it circular, too, and plant the trees and shrubs in a circular pattern that accentuates the design.

Enclosures

The edges of an enclosure usually produce a feeling of safety and security. However, a space that is too enclosed will create the uncomfortable sensation of being in a cage. Natural boundaries, such as canyon walls and

Left: The man-made angles in this garden match the natural geometry of the setting and provide a contrast to the loose forms of the plantings. Right: When planning a landscape, consider the various elements in terms of their form only. The contrasting forms of pond and plantings create a striking visual effect.

Right: Providing a sense of enclosure is an important objective of landscape design. This landscape gives a feeling of tranquility and privacy.
Below: The shade under mature trees provides welcome relief from the sun. When designing a landscape, remember to plan for both sun and shade areas.

Enclosure

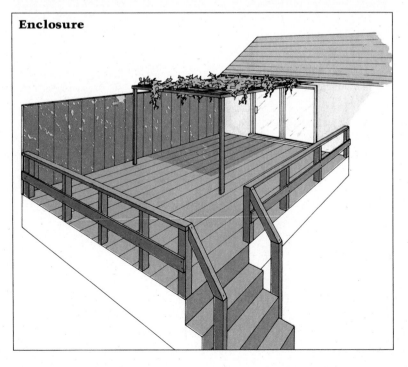

banks of foliage from trees and shrubs, enable the landscape to project a sense of security. Similar effects can be created by fences.

A space doesn't have to be enclosed to impart a feeling of protection and comfort. Enclosure may be created from something as simple as an umbrella tent or a gazebo. Low-mounding shrubs, a rock outcropping, or a depression in the earth caused by the roots of an old tree can seem protective, even though they do not formally enclose anything. Nor does enclosure have to exist from the level point of view. The boughs of a tree overhead or a trellised vine covering a patio can provide the sought-after security.

Enclosure does not actually have to provide safety to be effective. On a pier over water, a heavy chain running between 2-foot-tall bollards can provide a sense of security, when in reality it does little to ensure it. In the same way, the low guardrail along the outside edge of a treacherous mountain pass makes drivers feel safer.

Slopes

A landscape is significantly influenced by the slope of the ground. Natural or designed slopes affect the way areas are used and the available views. The practical considerations of drainage and grading are covered in the sixth chapter, "Installing Your Landscape."

Adding interest to a landscape, sloped surfaces often provide a sense of enclosure and tend to intensify the play of light, color, and shadow. On the other hand, if a slope gives the impression that something might fall on the viewer, it creates a negative sensation.

Even minor changes in incline can be very noticeable. A 3 percent grade (a ⅜-inch drop for every 12 inches of length) doesn't sound like much of a slope, but it is the maximum allowable on the interstate freeway system, even as it crosses the Sierra Nevada, the Rocky Mountains, and the Ozarks. Compared with level ground, a 3 percent slope can be as evident as a painting that is askew on a wall. When planned carefully, though, a slightly tilted plane can be appropriate, providing just a hint of enclosure. A battered surface is a wall that slopes away from the ground at an angle greater than 90 degrees. Battered surfaces reflect more light than simple vertical ones and appear solid and stable. Walls and

Planning a landscape around a naturally occurring slope requires some extra thought and effort, but is worth it. Slopes provide natural shape and add character to a garden.

hedges appear to have more solidity if they are given this shape.

Symbolism in Form

Many forms have deep-seated symbolic connotations. Vertical forms naturally draw attention and tend to induce a sense of awe. To capitalize on this feeling, plant a column of trees, place a slender statue in the garden where it will be shown off to advantage, or paint the high wall of a garage to exaggerate its height.

Diminutive and intricate forms, such as those in miniature gardens or the patterns in a detailed pavement design, tend to provoke curiosity. The static nature of a horizontal line, such as still waters, promotes feelings of peacefulness or passivity and gives the appearance of permanence.

Eighteenth-century garden designers believed that geometric forms composed of straight lines were the ultimate expression of

Slopes

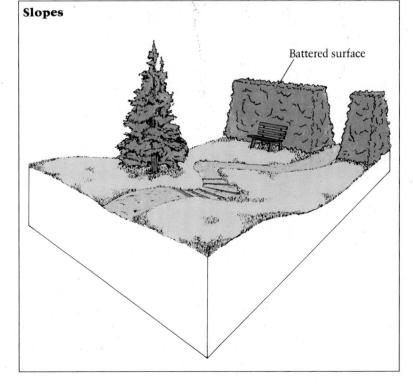

Battered surface

reason. A square lawn, a rectangular pattern made of box hedges, angled planting beds, a geometrically inventive patio—all have meaningful impact on a landscape.

Circular forms convey a feeling of closure, and, like islands or eddies in a stream, are complete in themselves. An entryway with a circular design implies that it is a place to wait. When the door opens, the circle is broken along the boundary of closure.

Curves are visual symbols of harmony. A garden has many curved shapes: leaves and pebbles, a billowing mass of foliage, a rolling terrace. When designing a paved walkway or the edges of a narrow planting bed, give them gentle, sweeping motions that flow from one to the other.

Projecting and jagged forms suggest dynamism and may imply speed and strength. Depending on how they are used, they may also merely look sloppy. Projecting forms can also imply power. A cantilevered deck, for instance, whose footings are invisible, seems to defy gravity.

Low, shelflike, covered forms, such as caves and canopied walks, imply protection. In contrast, the expansive desert under a starry sky can be oppressive in its openness, causing one to yearn for mountains or buildings that have the capacity to enclose. In a very broad, level site, the juxtaposition of open and covered spaces gives each a stronger identity.

THE ELEMENTS OF THE SENSES

Although the effects of a garden on the senses of touch, smell, and sight are often very subtle and difficult to define, they are elemental to an appreciation of the setting.

Microclimate

A microclimate is the fairly uniform climate in a locality or site. It may also be a pocket of modified climate within one site. Temperature, relative humidity, and wind determine climate. The importance of the microclimate cannot be overemphasized. In planning where to plant a shrub that requires full sun, where to build a deck, and even where to place major walkways, the nature of the microclimate will determine the success of a design.

The microclimate of a landscape is influenced by four factors: the presence or absence of direct sunlight, the temperature of the still air, the relative humidity, and the amount of wind. The outdoor comfort range generally lies between 70° and 80° F, as long as the relative humidity is between 20 and 50 percent, and the wind less than 3½ miles per hour.

The higher the humidity rises, the more unpleasant high temperatures become. Wind can reduce the effects of humid weather; however, where wind velocity exceeds about 3½ miles per hour, comfort diminishes. In a hot, humid climate, look for ways to provide areas that are shaded from the sun or ways to make the most of cooling breezes.

Strikingly different directions and velocities of wind occur at different elevations. The wind speed at 1 foot above the ground may be only half that at 6 feet above the ground. When the wind is obstructed, it will slow down even further. Even a 2-foot-high barrier can block most ground wind, a feature to keep in mind when planning a deck or patio in a windy location.

Because wind lowers temperatures and carries sound, get to know the wind patterns in the landscape to take advantage of summer breezes or to avoid winter turbulence, and to shield out certain sounds.

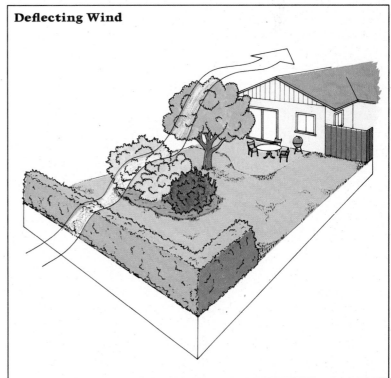

Deflecting Wind

Light and Shadow

The quality of light and shadow varies according to the sun's orientation to a site and the ability of the light to reach the ground. The amount of light a particular location receives during the course of a single day will greatly influence how the landscape should be designed. For a site that is too enclosed by tall trees, consider ways of allowing more filtered light. Observe the interplay of light and shadow: Size and temperature can be increased or decreased, and complexities of line and texture can be highlighted or deemphasized.

Illumination that strikes surfaces can be described as front, side, and back light. Front-lighting can reflect onto and brighten dark surfaces. Sidelighting heightens contrast and can produce silhouettes. The most dramatic backlighting occurs twice a day, when the sun rises and when it sets. Another example of backlighting is when the rays of the sun fall through a canopy of leaves. Backlighting is a popular technique used to illuminate a garden at night: Hidden lights cast a diffused glow behind foliage or objects of interest.

Also pay attention to shadow patterns caused by the house and trees. They can influence decisions about the positioning of sitting areas and the choices of construction materials and plants.

Sound

Sound can be conducted or carried depending on the needs of the situation. The splashing of a nearby stream or the rustling of a large tree, for example, may be highlighted by allowing an unobstructed flow of air from the stream or tree. Street noise, on the other hand, may be muffled by building solid fences or walls that will block the movement of sound. Unpleasant sounds can sometimes be masked with more musical ones.

Temperature

When cool air moves over land, it travels downward, from high to low elevations. Fog, a dramatic example of this process, can be seen flowing down mountainsides and collecting in valleys and canyons. Cool night air commonly becomes trapped in low pockets between hills

Left: One of the most striking lighting effects occurs when a canopy of leaves is backlit by the rays of the sun. Trees with light-colored foliage are particularly well-suited for backlighting.
Right: The sound of splashing water adds another dimension to the landscape. A simple waterfall masks the unpleasant noises from a neighboring street.

and buildings. If a house is near the bottom of a hill, it may be preferable to build a deck on the uphill side of the house, because the night air will be warmer than on the downhill side.

Correspondingly, warm air moves upward, from low to high elevations. To help an area retain warmth, provide surfaces that absorb heat during the day and release it at night. The heat of the sun can be best exploited by tilting surfaces at an angle perpendicular to the sun. A wall angled to collect direct sunlight will be warmer than an adjacent vertical wall. Solar panels are positioned to take advantage of this fact. Absorbed and reflected heat can noticeably warm the area surrounding the heat-retaining surface.

In choosing building materials for structures in a garden, take into account how much heat they retain. Stone, for example, retains considerable heat; wood retains heat moderately well; and fiberglass retains very little heat. Heat absorption is affected by other factors, as well. Dark materials absorb more heat than light-colored ones. Most natural materials absorb heat well.

When considering color in the landscape, don't overlook some of the more unusual combinations. Bright colors can be used to lighten, and contrast with, dark areas; subtle variations of the same color can engage the viewer; and bold texture and color contrasts can be fascinating to observe.

Color

Because color is a phenomenon of light, both the intensity of sunlight and the quality of shadow affect the reflectivity of color in a garden. On an overcast day, colors appear muted; on a bright, summer day, they seem vivid. These changes may affect mood, perhaps unconsciously: People feel depressed on a gray day and vivacious on a sunny one.

Colors also alter perspective. Light, cool colors enlarge space; dark, warm colors make areas appear smaller. Blue and gray seem farther away than dark green and red.

Fragrance

The nose, like the ears and eyes, is one way to perceive the landscape. If a site is affected by unpleasant odors, such as exhaust fumes from a busy street or the smell from a chicken coop, locate major activity areas upwind from them, if possible. Ephemeral scents, such as those of certain vines, shrubs, and trees, can help to camouflage offensive smells as well as add force to the landscape. Plan to place the most fragrant plants where they will do the most good. For instance, plant night-blooming nicotiana around a hot tub that is used at night, and honeysuckle by the front gate.

Texture

Fine textures such as lawns, mosses, and large, smooth pavements tend to accentuate the mass and shape of the ground and to increase its apparent size. These areas often act as a neutral screen or background for other textural elements placed on them—furnishings, sculpture, and even people.

Coarse textures such as cobbles, bricks, tufty grasses, herringbone decking, and redwood blocks or rounds draw attention to their

Above: Include plants with fragrant foliage and flowers, and place them where they will be enjoyed. Imagine the wonderful scent of roses that greets the visitor entering the garden by this front walk.
Right: The route to the front gate becomes much more enticing by using a curved path and unusual construction materials.

surfaces. For this reason, consider the range of textures to use in order to downplay or highlight the topography.

In planning textures, as in planning all other design elements, be clear in your intentions. Use coarse or fine textures and materials of strong color definition sparingly and dynamically. Avoid mixing too many textures in a single pavement area, but do allow special, intricate textures to stand out, or create areas with textural contrasts. Remember that fine-textured plants lose their distinctive quality if planted in the distant background. Similarly, coarse-textured plants may be too bold for close-up viewing. For the best effect, place plants where their textural qualities will be spotlighted. (See page 33 for a description of how to use contrasting textures to manipulate perspective.)

An area in a patio intended for barbecuing might be surfaced with smooth concrete, which is easy to clean, and the remainder of the patio could have an exposed aggregate surface that reflects less light and is more visually formal in keeping with its use as an outdoor living room.

Every texture contributes to the overall feeling in the landscape, so choose elements carefully. Subtle and pleasing combinations can be created by varying textures of plants, building materials, and dappled shade patterns cast by trees.

Plants and Materials

Selecting colors, textures, and materials is half the enjoyment of creating a landscape. When using plants, wood, masonry, and other readily available materials, the possibilities are endless.

Landscapes are made from various living and nonliving materials. Most people are familiar with the characteristics of construction materials—wood, stone, concrete, brick, and other substances—and can confidently select one or another based on appearance, suitability, and cost. But because of the diversity of available plants, some people feel less confident about choosing the ones needed to complete a landscape.

Familiarity with the plants that grow in your area will enable you to create a more unusual and functional landscape. Take note of appealing plants in other gardens. If necessary, ask the owner for the names of the plants, or take a small leaf sample to a local nursery or garden center for identification.

Research the plants that you like—their water, soil, fertilizer, and climate requirements; their natural form and mature size; whether they have an invasive root system, lose their leaves or drop fruit, or provide shade; or any other characteristic that might be important in a particular situation.

Gardening books provide a wealth of information on a wide variety of plants. A number of Ortho books can help you become familiar with all types of plant material. Some of these are *All About Trees, How to Select & Care for Shrubs & Hedges, All About Lawns, All About Ground Covers, Color With Annuals, All About Roses, All About Bulbs, The World of Cactus & Succulents, All About Perennials, Landscaping With Wildflowers & Native Plants,* and *All About Azaleas, Camellias & Rhododendrons.*

Subtle selection and placement of plants and constructed features (in this case, succulents and a reflecting pool) can create small areas of great beauty.

For more detailed information concerning the construction of fences, decks, patios, walkways, and other garden projects, use the Ortho books *How to Design & Build Decks & Patios, Garden Construction, How to Design & Build Fences & Gates, Basic Masonry Techniques,* and *How to Design & Install Outdoor Lighting.*

Important elements may already exist in a landscape. Study each and consider how it will fit in the future landscape design. Whether that element is the view from over a fence, the contours of the terrain, a mature tree, or a large outcropping of rocks, it can give a landscape character.

If you have recently moved into a previously owned home, especially an older one, the elements available for use in the landscape may not be readily apparent. In such cases, do not make rash changes in the garden for at least a year. Many new homeowners discover that they have at least a year's worth of work to do on the inside of the house. During this time, watch closely what surprises the garden reveals, and decide which should be incorporated into your plan.

When remodeling the garden right away, particularly during the dormant season, you may discover, too late, that you have destroyed a twenty-year-old bed of violets, peonies, or lilies of the valley. You may have ignored a dormant bed of nasturtiums that springs into vibrant life each year, or a thick tangle of branches that later becomes a mass of lilac blossoms. These special elements cannot always be easily replaced. In almost every case, size or established nature of the plants makes them a valued addition to the landscape.

APPROPRIATE PLANTS

One of the most important—and most often overlooked—aspects of choosing plant material is determining whether or not a plant is appropriate. The many appropriate choices for a particular spot depend on how well a plant fits your requirements and complements the landscape as a whole, and if it will be able to grow to maturity in the location where it is placed. For example, an Arizona cypress (*Cupressus glabra*) or a giant dracaena palm (*Cordyline australis*) may be appealing, but both may look out of place in an area that is planted predominantly with deciduous trees and broadleaf evergreens. Moreover, the climatic conditions in a landscape may be less than optimum for these choices.

The goal in choosing plants for a landscape is to create a willing garden, one that embraces and nurtures the plants within it. Above all, use plants whose characteristics you like—their flowers, forms, fall colors, or other features—but make sure the plants are well-suited to the environment.

It is much easier to find examples of inappropriate use of plants in a landscape than examples of appropriate use. Instances of inappropriate use include the residence that cuts itself off from "borrowed views" with an unnecessary planting of trees along the property line, thereby reinforcing the smallness of the property; tropical plants that should be grown in a greenhouse but are kept alive with tents and heaters during the yearly cold spell; the lawn that is never used for play or sitting, but must still be watered, fertilized, mowed, and raked; the giant forest tree planted on the south side of the patio or pool where it blocks the sun; the fruit tree that drops rotting fruit on a well-traveled pathway; the water-loving

The appropriate use of plants is central to the success of any landscape. A variety of plants can be used together if they are appropriate to the setting and compatible with each other.

plants under the drought-loving tree, which is failing because it is overwatered; and the monotony of a common palette of plants or the spotty and weak look of too many different plants, paving materials, and forms, all out of balance. Plants used appropriately are much less easy to recognize simply because they blend naturally into their setting. An awareness of appropriate plant selection and use will help to create an attractive and healthy garden that suits your needs.

FLOORS FOR THE LANDSCAPE

Since most people can easily think of outdoor space in terms of interior space, the discussion of materials can be divided into three categories: "floors," including steps and walkways; "ceilings," including branching trees, overhead lattice work, and other overhead enclosures; and "walls," including shrubs, trees, fences, and other garden dividers.

The first thing to choose in a landscape design should be the "carpeting" for the outdoor "rooms." The color, texture, and pattern of a good garden floor covering should blend with the other elements in the landscape. Materials can be selected for their ease of maintenance as well, but, above all, they should be visually pleasing.

Living Choices

The many possibilities for living floor coverings include a broad range of colors, textures, maintenance requirements, costs, and other important considerations.

Lawns Of the many living ground coverings, grass lawns have been the favorite of generations of gardeners. A carpet of even, closely clipped greenery does more than just provide a level surface for various activities. As a unifying element, a lawn may tie together many different aspects of the garden. Lawns often are used to simulate a meadow surrounded by or interspersed with flowers, trees, and other apparently naturally occurring plants. In areas where there are few meadows because of summer drought, lawns are generally inappropriate. Consider alternatives to save water and maintenance. Lawns in particular and ground covers in general require some amount of upkeep throughout the year.

Ground covers These popular flooring plants include cotoneaster and wild lilac (*Ceanothus* species), which, when used as carpeting, produce a less tailored look than lawns or finer-textured ground covers. Other choices are ivy (*Hedera* species), pachysandra, star jasmine (*Trachelospermum jasminoides*),

Left: Many native floor coverings can be brought into the garden to provide color and to create a natural-looking setting. This attractive mix of woodland ground covers and flowers gives the impression of untamed nature. Right: When evaluating choices for ground covers, the most important consideration is whether the area will receive much foot traffic. Particularly tender plants, such as baby's tears (pictured), are attractive to look at but require clearly defined paths to avoid being damaged.

blue fescue grass, dusty miller (*Senecio cineraria*), sedum, asparagus fern (*Asparagus* species), mounding bougainvillea, bergenia, ferns, and naturalized wildflowers.

Natural balance As you plan and plant ground covers, remember that the ground surface in its natural state is seldom completely overlaid with vegetation, but is a mosaic composed of the various plants that make up the local plant community. Basic components of natural ground covers include rock outcroppings, boulders, and open patches of exposed soil. Observe areas of natural ground cover and plan your landscape design accordingly. Ground covers, once they are well established, help to keep out weeds and can delineate areas of the garden, as well as add color, form, fragrance, and contrast.

If low maintenance is desirable, choose hardy plant varieties and also consider man-made materials.

Nonliving Materials

Keep in mind that solid, nonliving surfaces require good drainage; some, like untextured concrete, can be slippery when wet. Because solid surfaces can cut off the supply of air and water to the soil, they should not be laid too close to the trunks of trees or large shrubs.

Gravel An important material for "instant" landscaping, gravel can provide immediate, inexpensive flooring in a garden. It can look informal, or appear formal and austere, as in the traditional French garden with its long, narrow, gravel-filled paths. Gravel is easy to install but usually needs constant upkeep with a rake to clean it of leaves, twigs, and other debris. To help gravel stay in place, construct raised boundaries using headers (see page 103) around it, made of 2 by 4 lumber, brick, or other materials. Another alternative is to set the gravel in asphalt or concrete that has been laid over black plastic, weed prevention fabric, or sterilized soil (see pages 81 and 82) to prevent seeds from germinating and poking through the surface. Roll the gravel to create a composite.

Concrete Slabs of concrete make a popular, practical, and adaptable material for patio construction, and are the most economical of

Above: Using unusual ground covers in new combinations will create surprising visual effects. Consider the color, shape, and texture of the adjacent constructed surfaces when planning the garden floor.
Left: A ground covering of rocks or gravel is generally a permanent addition to the landscape. The low cost, ease of installation, and the ability to withstand heavy use are some of the advantages of this type of covering.

Left: Wooden decks have the distinct advantage of being able to create a level surface over uneven terrain. The natural quality of the deck material blends in well with almost any style of landscape. Right: Shaded, damp areas require special attention and planning. Here, rough stone, laid in an attractive, rounded pattern, provides secure footing. Small flower beds add color and contrast to the stone.

all paved surfaces. Concrete can be cold and look monotonous if it is not relieved by contrasting materials. Popular ways to add color and texture to concrete are to inlay it with stone, intersperse it with planter beds, or make geometric patterns by combining concrete, brick, and wood.

Wood Another common and popular building material, wood is most often thought of in relation to decks. A wooden deck is generally about twice as expensive to construct as a concrete surface. Decks, unlike concrete or brick patios, do not have to be built on level land and can be placed in just about any appropriate location. Be sure that the deck, the steps leading to and from it, and the surrounding walks are related in some way. This can be accomplished by making wood the motif that ties the parts together. For example, railroad ties can be used for steps and tree rounds for walkways.

To learn in detail about deck planning and construction and about concrete and other types of patios, see Ortho's book *How to Design & Build Decks & Patios.*

Stones Another choice for an outdoor floor, stones may be somewhat unkind to bare feet. When stones are laid in a bed of sand, their color and texture enliven a landscape. This method of flooring works well around trees and large shrubs, because air and water can circulate through the sand base. Special stones may be used as accents, and although they are more expensive than gravel or concrete, fewer will be needed to create an attractive effect.

Tiles Used for a terrace or a patio, tiles are especially suitable in a Mediterranean-style garden. The tiles should be unglazed, since glazed tiles are extremely slippery when wet. Clay tiles blend in with both rustic and formal landscapes. However, concrete tiles, even when installed in a pattern, are easier to lay than clay tiles. Clay tiles have to be carefully laid on a concrete bed, over absolutely level terrain, and then mortared together, whereas concrete tiles can simply be placed in a level bed of gravel and sand.

Bricks Incorporated into the garden, bricks are an especially versatile material. They may be used either formally as a solid surface, or informally, in a zigzag pattern. A house need not be made of brick for a brick walkway or patio to look attractive. By providing shape, color, and textural interest, bricks can unify almost any garden.

Plants and constuction materials can be used together attractively for practical purposes. Wild strawberries and potted marigolds brighten this stone stair.

Recycled materials Many nonliving landscaping materials recycle well. Broken pieces of concrete make good retaining walls or stepping-stones. Even a patio can be constructed from such pieces by laying them in sand with 2-inch spaces between them, in which low plants such as chamomile or creeping thyme are planted. Weathered fencing or shed boards also recycle well, if they do not look too unkempt, and their weathered character adds a softening effect to new construction. Old bricks are invaluable assets that provide an appearance of order without being overly cold and formal.

Steps and walkways Any nonliving outdoor flooring material can be used to construct steps and walkways. Ideally, however, they should be made of materials that complement those found elsewhere in the landscape. In a location with a brick terrace, brick can be used to edge concrete steps and paths. A walkway adjoining a concrete patio might look best with an exposed aggregate surface, or perhaps with something as simple as gray gravel.

To avoid creating an overwhelming effect, do not use too much of the same material throughout the landscape. On the other hand, to prevent visual confusion, do not mix too many unrelated materials in the same area. The key word is balance: The overall scene should be harmonious.

CEILINGS FOR THE LANDSCAPE

The most beautiful ceiling for outdoor rooms is usually the sky. Although most outdoor space is open to the elements, a landscape should have places that are protected from the sun, rain, and wind.

Trees

When asked to devise ideas for ceilings, many people think of the canopy of leaves created by a large, overhanging tree. Trees provide cooling protection from the sun, while having appeal for their size, texture, and ever-changing pattern of their leaves.

In selecting new trees or analyzing mature ones in the landscape, learn the habits of the trees in question: their mature height, spread, form, texture, color, leaf fall and winter appearance, flowers, fragrance, fruit, rate of growth, hardiness, pest problems, potential life span, transplanting and pruning requirements, and any additional maintenance information.

The most satisfactory trees are those that thrive in the natural conditions of a yard. If ease of maintenance is important, choose species that adapt best to the particular site and fill specific design requirements. As common names for many plants vary, botanical names are listed for most trees so that you can find them in reference books or at a local nursery or arboretum. Ortho's book *All About Trees* will help you make the best choice.

Broadleaf evergreens These trees retain their leaves the year around, losing a percentage of them seasonally, but never all of them at one time. Examples are the olive (*Olea europaea*), pittosporum, live oak (several species of *Quercus*), eucalyptus, frangipani, acacia, tamarisk, camphor (*Cinnamomum camphora*), and magnolia. Individual species may have special features worth noting, such as flowers, fragrance, fruit, or particularly distinctive forms.

Coniferous trees Characterized by scaly or needlelike leaves and bearing cones, coniferous trees are woody plants. This group includes the redwood (*Sequoia sempervirens*), pine (*Pinus* species), juniper (*Juniperus* species), yew (*Taxus* species), larch (*Larix* spe-

cies), fir (*Abies* species), spruce (*Picea* species), hemlock (*Tsuga* species), arborvitae (*Thuja* species), cypress (*Cupressus* species), and false cypress (*Chamaecyparis* species). There are a few deciduous conifers, such as the dawn redwood (*Metasequoia glyptostroboides*) from China and the southeastern bald cypress (*Taxodium distichum*), but for the most part, conifers retain their foliage from two to seven years, losing from one half to one seventh of the total each year. The major needle loss occurs in the fall months.

Deciduous trees   These trees lose all or most of their leaves seasonally. Some species are only semideciduous in regions that are not cold enough to force them into full dormancy. This climatic factor often causes deciduous trees to perform less well in areas that lack seasonally cold weather. For instance, the Chinese pistachio (*Pistacia chinensis*) will have better leaf color where a distinct cold snap occurs in the fall than in warmer areas where fall weather comes on more gradually.

Some examples of deciduous trees are the pin oak (*Quercus palustris*), walnut, aspen (*Populus tremuloides*), apple, cherry, willow (*Salix* species), ash (*Fraxinus* species), sycamore (*Platanus* species), chestnut (*Castanea* species), and redbud (*Cercis* species). The special features of deciduous trees are their fall colors, their bare winter form, and their flowers, fragrance, and fruit. Deciduous trees provide summer shade, but also allow the winter sun to warm what lies beneath or behind them—a quality that should be taken into consideration in many sites.

Exotic trees   Trees native to either the tropics or the desert are considered exotic in most regions of the country, and will grow willingly only in warm areas. These diverse types include the date palm (*Phoenix* species), tree fern (*Dicksonia* and other genera), monkeypod (*Samanea saman*), albizzia, Joshua (*Yucca brevifolia*), cajeput (*Melaleuca quinquenervia)*, and ironwood (*Mesua ferrea*).

When the climate allows for the use of these trees, they can create an impression of lush tropics or a desert oasis, or can accent the landscape as living sculptures.

Plastic and Fiberglass

Synthetic materials are usually less aesthetically pleasing than natural materials for use in the garden. However, translucent fiberglass or plastic panels overhead can ensure complete privacy from upstairs windows; soften the light; and, when viewed from underneath, provide interesting patterns from overhanging tree limbs. The wooden struts over which the material is laid also cast pleasing shadows.

A synthetic ceiling may be an ideal covering for semitropical plants because it creates

Right: While canvas may not be the most durable of all outdoor ceilings, the crisp, traditional look cannot be matched.

Above: A wooden overhead, with space left between the slats, offers a pleasing balance of light and shade. The open structure allows maximum air circulation.
Right: A lattice overhead, painted a light color, has a refined, formal appearance. Lattice is easy to construct and relatively inexpensive.

an environment that has the effect of a greenhouse. The greatest virtues of plastic, fiberglass, and similar sheltering materials are their simplicity and economy.

Canvas

The festivity of a circus tent or the crispness of a nautical scene can be created with canvas. Canvas can be dismantled and stored at the first sign of rain or snow. When spring arrives, it can be reattached to its frame. In windy areas, canvas can be used for panels that act as windbreaks. A canvas shelter can also be made into a gazebo, and at less expense than one made of lath. An appealing quality of canvas is that light glows softly through it. In time, though, the sun and the elements will cause canvas to wear out and it will need replacing.

Wood and Reeds

The best of both sun and shade can be utilized when an open area is designed next to a sheltered one. Solid overhead structures provide complete shade, but trap warm air, resulting in a lack of ventilation. That could make the enclosure uninviting.

Rolls of bamboo screening or wooden slats pitched tent-fashion will filter the sunshine and create shadow patterns on the ground underneath. A lattice has a similar though more dramatic effect.

WALLS FOR THE LANDSCAPE

Among the many possibilities for outdoor walls and partial walls, the only common characteristic is that they are vertical. Outdoor walls can be formed from trees, hedges, shrubs, brick, wood, and other materials. Hedge walls can be loose and billowy for a casual look, or dense and tightly sheared for a more formal effect. Walls made from green plants, though architecturally neutral, are more romantic than solid, nonplant walls, and are also less expensive and forbidding.

Although partial walls may consist of permanent structures or plantings, they tend to look airier and lighter than full walls. Partial walls are often designed to be versatile, such as shades that can be rolled up or down to regulate the amount of privacy or protection from sun and wind.

Shrubs

Like trees, shrubs are woody plants. In general, shrubs have more than one stem or trunk, and are smaller than 15 feet when mature. The distinction between small trees and large shrubs is not definitive, and the two terms are often used interchangeably. Shrubs range from broadleaf and coniferous evergreens to deciduous and exotic varieties.

Broadleaf evergreen shrubs   These include the fire thorn (*Pyracantha* species), rhododendron, abelia, camellia, aucuba, bottlebrush (*Callistemon* species), boxwood (*Buxus* species), and privet (*Ligustrum* species). Broadleaf evergreen shrubs, which are among the most versatile plants in the landscape, can be used for enclosures, screens, and barriers, and are often notable for their form, fragrance, color, and fruit.

Deciduous shrubs   Examples are the forsythia, redbud (*Cercis* species), quince (*Chaenomeles* species), dogwood (*Cornus florida* and some other species), hazelnut (*Corylus* species), sumac (*Rhus glabra* and other species), rose, lilac (*Syringa* species),

hydrangea, and elderberry (*Sambucus* species). In cold climates, deciduous shrubs make excellent texture and color contrasts when massed with evergreen shrubs.

Coniferous shrubs   Some attractive possibilities include the juniper (*Juniperus* species), yew (*Taxus* species), Japanese black pine (*Pinus thunbergiana*), weeping blue spruce (*Picea pungens* 'Pendens'), and dwarf or semidwarf forms of coniferous trees.

Tropical and desert shrubs   Examples include the Chinese hibiscus (*Hibiscus rosa-sinensis*), fatsia, fuchsia, plumbago, jasmine (*Jasminum* and *Trachelospermum* species), gardenia, tobira (*Pittosporum tobira*), oleander (*Nerium oleander*), Natal plum (*Carissa grandiflora*), and sweet olive (*Osmanthus fragrans*).

Shrubs can serve as partitions in outdoor room areas if they are not planted too close together and are left unsheared. They can be evergreen or deciduous, flowering or nonflowering varieties. A deciduous variety might be appropriate if a tall shrub is required to screen an undesirable view. When the shrub

Left: To keep an even appearance, this needled evergreen requires selective pruning rather than shearing. Hedges are among the most appropriate of all garden walls, and provide a lush background for other plants.
Right: Vines can cover a vertical surface completely, creating the look of a hedge.

loses its leaves in the winter, it will still function as a screen while allowing the low, winter sun to reach the part of the garden that otherwise might not get much natural light. The bare skeletons of shrubs in the winter can be sculpturally pleasing.

Vines

Extremely versatile plants, vines creep, trail, crawl, climb, and bring color, fragrance, richness, and variety to an outdoor setting. Some vines, such as bougainvillea, also make good ground covers. Vines will soften the effect of a fence or any solid structure and can themselves be used as living walls or screens.

A climbing rose, such as *Rosa banksiae* (sometimes called 'Lady Banks'), makes a loose, informal wall. A clinging vine, such as creeping fig (*Ficus pumila*), can attach itself to a fence or the back of a garage, becoming a crisp, flat covering that provides an evenly textured green mat. Clematis vines, although deciduous, offer some of the most beautiful blossoms possible. Jasmines are popular vines, and many varieties add a wonderful scent to the garden, in addition to having attractive flowers. The bounteous blooms of wisteria, the most romantic of all the vines, can hang over the top of a fence or garland a wall. Before choosing a vine, though, make sure that it is not overly invasive or so fast growing that it might cause problems later.

Vines have several methods for holding on to vertical surfaces: disks or suction cups (Virginia creeper—*Parthenocissus quinquefolia*); aerial roots (philodendron); twining stems, in which the leaders grow around the supports (wisteria); tendril coils (passion vine—*Passiflora* species); leafstalk coils (nasturtium—*Tropaeolum majus*); and thorns (climbing roses and berries). Many other plants can be artificially supported to give the effect of vines by affixing them to upright stakes and other vertical surfaces. The way a vine grows is important in deciding which one to choose. Two key factors in selecting vines are whether they will ever need to be removed and what kind of surface (texture and strength) they will adhere to.

Above: Many varieties of roses are natural climbers, suitable for use on walls and fences. Below right: An open, vine-covered lattice has been used to screen a parking area. Below left: Shrubs placed against walls will soften and add color to them.

Screens

An inexpensive reed screen, available in a roll, can be quickly erected to make an effective partial wall. Flexible and easy to work with, this kind of screening generally lends itself to an informal setting, but can also blend into a small, formal oriental garden. Reed screening wears out, however, and needs replacing every two to three years.

Concrete Blocks

More expensive and permanent than reed screening is a wall or partial wall made of concrete blocks. Available in a range of patterns, styles, and colors, concrete blocks can be employed to create a variety of geometric openwork in patterned walls that ensure both privacy and air circulation. One or two carefully chosen designs can be used by themselves or in combination with solid blocks. To guarantee the solidity and permanence of a wall of concrete blocks, set them in mortar.

Trellises

Perhaps the most handsome man-made screens are trellises. Often used in formal French gardens, they can also have a rustic or modern effect, depending on the pattern chosen and whether or not the wood is rough or finished. Trellising can create a feeling of enclosure and privacy without blocking the sun and breeze and without eliminating the view. Trellis patterns also add a vertical or horizontal element to a garden. Some of the most attractive trellises are those partially covered with vines.

Fences

In addition to providing privacy, supporting vines, protecting against strong winds, creating comfortably warm spots in sunny areas, adding horizontal or vertical form, and meeting many other needs, fences can unify a house and garden when they are made of a material that is harmonious with both.

Steel If security is necessary around a house, erect a chain-link fence, but disguise it with vines or a hedge, or camouflage it by painting it a dark, natural color. A fence should be as attractive on one side as on the other, so before constructing any type of fence, consult your neighbors.

Wood Choose a style of wood fence appropriate to the setting. For example, for a Colonial house, a picket fence is appropriate. These and some other styles can be bought in ready-made sections; the more elaborate fences are handmade.

If a house has clapboard siding, a fence made of the same material and constructed in the same manner is a good choice. The horizontal lines of a clapboard fence can be softened with plantings of shrubs, vines, or trees.

Large lumberyards and building supply stores often display short sections of a variety of wooden fence styles from which to choose or draw inspiration.

Whether rustic or formal, fences provide visual interest in addition to being practical barriers in the garden. Choose one that fits both the needs and style of the setting.

Above: Natural walls will change with the seasons, sometimes significantly altering landscape views. Here, the bare trees allow an open view, while the fog creates a dramatic, seasonal wall in the distance. Below: Foundation plantings hide the tall foundations of many older homes.

Iron   If a house has a formal French style or is a Victorian gingerbread, the privacy of a solid fence can be sacrificed for the security and handsome appearance of an ornamental wrought-iron fence.

Brick   Brick can be used to create solid or open fences. For a sturdy yet open fence, brick pillars can be placed at strategic intervals and joined with iron or wood in an open pattern—in contrast to using walls of solid brick.

FOUNDATION PLANTING

This style of planting is usually characterized by an assortment of entirely or predominantly evergreen shrubs placed to hide the foundation and basement structures of houses. Foundation planting developed during the Victorian period, when first-floor basements were common and homeowners wished to disguise them. It was also used around bungalow houses constructed across the United States in the early twentieth century. Foundation planting is now commonly seen around modern ranch-style houses—not always appropriate because the plantings chosen often are too large for the setting and, as they grow, will cover windows, blocking light and views.

Use of only two or three harmonious species, or even a single species, rather than a hodgepodge that competes with the house for attention, can create a unified effect. Soft, but not oversized or unkempt, shrubs of contrasting textures provide more grace and appeal than the rigid, carefully shaped shrubs common to traditional foundation planting.

Flowering shrubs are best chosen to complement the colors of the house and its foundation. For instance, most reds, pinks, and roses do not show well when placed against a bright brick backdrop.

Consider how the current landscape uses foundation planting, and whether or not that style fits the house. For an older bungalow or Victorian house, consider refurbishing the surroundings by accentuating the architectural style. Especially when there is a basic style to work with, a restored foundation planting can be very charming and elegant.

ACCENTS IN THE LANDSCAPE

Plants and other elements in the landscape do not always fall neatly into the structural categories of floors, ceilings, and walls. Accents such as specimen plants, colorful beds of flowers, sculptures, and other structures can be used to modify, strengthen, or otherwise enhance the basic form and design of a garden. Plants used as accents should be selected for their fine or unusual features. They generally look best when planted together, in small groups or in masses. Carefully plan the use of these plantings. Too many different accents in a small area can look like a botanical garden or nursery, instead of a well-designed landscape. Try planting them in masses, so that their colors, forms, or other unique qualities will be emphasized. When using an accent alone, place simpler vegetation around it.

When selecting accent plants, aim for understatement. If a section of the yard is planted with only one type of shrub, strikingly contrasting plants may be the appropriate choice. If four or five different shrubs with different colors, textures, and forms are planted in the same area, cautiously add accent plants to avoid visual confusion.

When accent plants are massed together, even when there are a number of varieties, they can form an oasis. To achieve the best effect, an oasis should be surrounded by areas of extreme simplicity. A natural oasis exists within flat, sandy areas, but this simplicity can also be created with mosses or other fine-textured plants. Cacti and other succulents make excellent oasis landscapes.

Cacti and Other Succulents

The many forms of succulents, including the cactus, are striking when used appropriately. These desert plants with their sometimes bizarre shapes and colors have gained and lost popularity several times in the United States since the 1880s, and are currently in vogue.

Some examples of cactus plants and other succulents are the echeveria, lapidaria, Christmas cactus (*Schlumbergera bridgesii*), agave, aloe, yucca, crassula, euphorbia, sedum, and dudleya. To learn more about how to choose, grow, and use them in a landscape, see Ortho's book *The World of Cactus & Succulents.*

Annuals, Biennials, And Perennials

The many annuals, biennials, and perennials are grown primarily for their colorful flowers in many forms.

Annuals These flowering plants grow from seed to maturity in one year and then die. In choosing where and when to use annuals, remember that they need yearly replacement and the constant care that new plants require. Because of their ephemeral quality, annuals make excellent container plants. Be sure to put them where their splashes of color, strong fragrances, and fast-growing forms will have a dramatic impact. In areas with mild climates, annual plantings can be rotated so that they provide color in the garden in almost every season.

Left: Succulents have some of the most unusual forms of any plants. Unique as accent plants, succulents are especially attractive when several species are combined for a contrasting effect. Right: Annuals provide a quick-growing display of color wherever you need it the most. Because they can be changed with the seasons, they are ideal accent plants.

Biennials and Perennials

Compared with perennials, which need at least three seasons to grow, biennials complete their life cycle in two seasons. Since biennials and perennials are more permanent plantings than annuals, it is important to organize the way they are laid out. Tremendously varied in form, size, and horticultural requirements, biennials and perennials are favorites in gardeners' gardens. The classic style of perennial borders, featured in English cottage gardens (see page 26), has been refined over the years into a gardening art.

Bulbs

Unlike other plants, these flowering plants have fleshy or enlarged underground stems, which store food during the dormant period. Corms, tubers, tuberous roots, and rhizomes also fall under the general category of bulb. Most bulbs blossom from 12 to 26 weeks after they are planted. The waiting period makes the gardener feel surprised and delighted when bulbs begin to come up.

Bulbs include daffodils, tulips, and narcissus; corms include freesias and gladiolus; tubers include gloxinias (*Sinningia* species) and tuberous begonias (*Begonia tuber-hybrida*); tuberous roots include dahlias, ranunculus, and anemone; and rhizomatous plants include bearded iris and canna.

Fungi

Tree and ground mosses, lichens, mushrooms, and other forms of fungi should not be over-

looked as part of a landscape planting. Use these unique plants where they will add a special element of interest.

A famous garden in Kyoto, Japan, features numerous varieties of mosses. Rock outcroppings in many natural areas are covered with colorful lichens. Clusters of mushrooms, although not always edible, are certainly enjoyable to discover in a garden. The Spanish moss of the deep South hangs from trees in unkempt, hoary threads, contributing greatly to the atmosphere of the region. The parasitic mistletoe that grows on many oak and walnut trees, although unhealthy for the trees, adds a distinctive statement to the landscape.

Above left: A bright yellow flower interplanted with parsley creates a striking contrast of color and texture. Above right: Bulbs bloom annually and are available in a wide variety of colors, shapes, and sizes. Left: Many fruits and vegetables have colors and forms that make them attractive accents in the garden. Parsley and cabbage, planted in a raised bed made of railroad ties, make a pleasing composition of contrasting shades of green.

Vegetables

As unusual ornamentals, vegetables can be striking additions to the landscape, as well as supplying an edible harvest. Ornamental cabbage (sometimes called kale) makes a handsome ground cover or annual border. Corn and sunflowers can act as accents or bold barriers. Peas and beans are quick-growing annual vines. Swiss chard provides outstanding color. Artichokes offer a perennial contrast in texture and color.

Berries

This delightful group of vines has several distinct uses. They make good barriers, as well as mounding ground covers. Wild blackberries are often viewed as the scourge of the garden, but when given enough space to grow naturally, they can be very attractive.

Structural Accents

Some of the most time-honored accents in the landscape are not plants but man-made structures; garden pools, pergolas and arbors, gazebos, ornamental containers, sculpture, and garden furniture are among the most common.

Structural accents, like plant accents, should be used with restraint. A pair of ornamental containers or a single gazebo is usually all the average-sized garden landscape can handle. Not all landscapes require an accent, but if one is used be sure to place it so that it receives the attention it deserves.

If a garden has symmetrical features, such as a path along an axis, consider placing a piece of sculpture along or at the terminus of the path, or where paths intersect where it will draw the eye (see page 34).

Before adding structural accents, consider the style of the landscape. Because of their prominence, these accents should be chosen with a careful eye for appropriateness and authenticity.

For the strongest effect use structural accents sparingly, and place them where they will receive the most attention. They may be both aesthetic and practical.

The Design Process

Making a plan is the all-important step in landscaping. While the plan is on paper, it can be changed without wasting a nickel. No matter how sketchy or professional a drawing is, it will help save both time and money.

Landscape plans are really a form of shorthand—an easy and effective way of noting ideas. A workable design cannot be made without a plan. A design develops as ideas are recorded, studied, and improved. You can take notes, study photographs and drawings of other landscapes, and make drawings of original ideas. All are intermediate steps to finding a design solution. The more possibilities you consider, the closer you will be to an effective design.

Landscape designs can be drawn freehand or with the aid of mechanical drafting tools. Whichever method is used, the plan will need to have correct scale in order to ensure accuracy when figuring the amount of soil amendments, ground-cover plants, trees, shrubs, and other materials the garden will need.

The bare, undeveloped site around a newly built house presents an ideal design opportunity for the home landscaper. Here, existing mature trees lend character and serve as a starting point, while the steep slope poses challenges in planning drainage and planting.

The materials and tools needed to produce professional working drawings may not be as extensive, or expensive, as you think. Everything you need is pictured here. See page 67 for a list of supplies.

DRAWING METHODS AND SUPPLIES

One very helpful tool is the architect's scale, which calibrates dimensions directly into the correct scale. For example, if a drawing uses proportions where ¼ inch equals 1 foot, the architect's scale will represent a 7-foot length as 1¾ inches long. Even if the plan is to be drawn freehand, invest in this tool—it will save many times its cost in time and effort.

Many aspects of a landscape plan can be successfully drawn freehand, but certain drafting tools, such as triangles and circle templates, will be helpful in making uniform angles and circles.

Choose a circle template that can draw circles from ½ to 3 inches in diameter. This tool is very useful for laying out planting and irrigation systems. Even if the landscape does not have circular details, it will be helpful in drawing circles to symbolize forms—for example, to represent the approximate spread of a particular plant. This approximation, based on the anticipated mature growth of the plant, is the easiest way to determine how many shrubs or trees are needed to make a mass planting. To find out the number of ground cover plants to put in a given area, take the square footage of the space and divide it by the footage requirement of each variety of ground cover.

Graph paper, used as the drawing surface, can be attached to a flat table with drafting tape. Drafting tape is like masking tape except that it can be removed without tearing the paper. Be sure the graph paper is lined to scale—for example, if the plan uses ¼ inch to represent 1 foot, buy graph paper with ¼-inch squares. Graph paper is available in various scales at most art supply stores. Art supply stores also carry tracing paper to place over the base plan for experimental drawings, also called bubble plans. Read about making a bubble plan on pages 71 and 72. Tracing paper comes in rolls as well as sheets. The best buy is a 12- or 14-inch roll of yellow or white flimsy—a thin tracing paper that is ideal for quick overlays and sketches.

For early freehand sketches, a soft lead pencil, marked B or F, is best. Harder pencils, such as H or 2H, are more suitable for fine-line drafting on working drawings.

When drafting plans, don't get too entranced by the drafting equipment. Triangles, templates, and other items can be helpful tools, but they should not overly influence the creation of the design.

For the working-drawing plan, more technical drafting tools, including a drafting board and T-square, may be appropriate because they can help produce professional-looking drawings.

Regardless of your background in drafting, satisfactory drawings can be made with basic equipment and a little practice. If your interest in drafting grows more than you anticipated, take advantage of this enthusiasm—the more thought-out and detailed the landscaping plan is, the more easily the actual construction can be implemented.

There are four basic steps in the design process: base plans, bubble plans, concept plans, and working plans. Base plans record all the primary information of a site. Bubble plans are rough sketches mapping out general ideas for the various uses of each part of the site. Concept plans clarify the bubble plans, taking each of the general functions or ideas

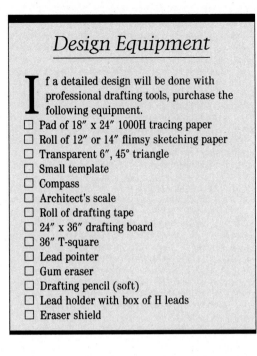

Design Equipment

If a detailed design will be done with professional drafting tools, purchase the following equipment.

☐ Pad of 18″ x 24″ 1000H tracing paper
☐ Roll of 12″ or 14″ flimsy sketching paper
☐ Transparent 6″, 45° triangle
☐ Small template
☐ Compass
☐ Architect's scale
☐ Roll of drafting tape
☐ 24″ x 36″ drafting board
☐ 36″ T-square
☐ Lead pointer
☐ Gum eraser
☐ Drafting pencil (soft)
☐ Lead holder with box of H leads
☐ Eraser shield

and giving them a specific form. For example, what was sketched in the bubble plan as an outside eating area becomes in the concept plan a deck or patio with built-in barbecue and benches. Working plans, further refinements of concept plans, include specific measurements, proportions, materials, building techniques, and other details important to the actual implementation of the design.

THE BASE PLAN

Before beginning to plan and design in earnest, it is necessary to know as much exact information about the site as possible. Features to record on paper include the dimensions of the site, existing plantings, walkways, fences, walls, slopes, outbuildings, and other significant characteristics.

Creating a new landscape from the present one requires translating the existing three-dimensional landscape into an accurate two-dimensional base plan of the property. The base plan will be an invaluable aid for design; not only will it record the details of the current landscape and make their relationships clear, but it will also make it easier to visualize any changes and additions.

Perhaps an existing base plan of the site can be obtained from the builder or architect, a former owner, or the city building department. If so, use it instead of drawing a plan, but look for three things: Make sure that it is

drawn correctly; check to see that whatever is indicated on the plan is still part of the landscape; and incorporate any new objects or plantings into the plan.

Making a base plan has additional benefits. The task of measuring the site will probably disclose rarely visited corners of the yard. Often, the most remote areas of a site present the most striking and seldom-seen views, exaggerate the size of the lot, or offer a certain amount of peace and solitude unavailable in the more traveled parts of the landscape. When exploring these areas, keep an open mind for the best ways to capitalize on their unique qualities.

The following pages will show how to make a base plan.

Scale

To determine which scale to choose, consider the information to be portrayed. A small space with many details needs a large scale, such as 1 inch to 1 foot. If the site is very large, a scale of 1 inch to 20 feet may be required in order to fit the entire site onto a single sheet of paper. If a larger scale is used, the drawing can be divided over more than one sheet. Indicate the scale somewhere on the plan itself—for example, "¼ inch = 1 foot."

To depict the normal residential landscape (½-acre lot or less), the recommended scale is ¼ inch to 1 foot, written as "1:4 scale." An

An architect's scale is simple to use and is a helpful tool for anyone designing and planning a landscape. To keep the plan in scale, consider purchasing this tool even if you intend to draw all your plans freehand.

Base Plan

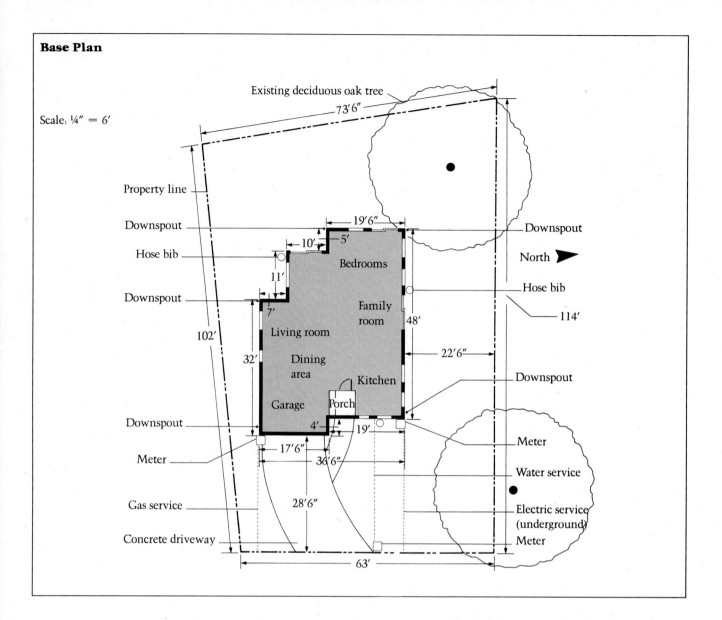

existing plan of the site can be adjusted to a ¼-inch scale by measuring and copying the plan onto another sheet.

Begin with a datum, also called a baseline. The baseline is the reference point from which all other measurements are taken. If the site is adjacent to a building, one of the walls of that building can serve as the baseline. If the site is in the open, where there are no existing baselines, use one edge of the property. A string tied between two stakes can also be employed to set up a straight line.

Draw the baseline near to one edge of the drafting paper and allow enough room on the paper to render the entire site. Always draw the plan with north at the top or on the left side of the paper; this standard practice will help building inspectors and others reading the plan to orient themselves to the site.

What to Include in the Plan

Work across the landscape with a 50- or 100-foot tape measure, making note of the location of everything that seems important. Include any of the following fixed objects in the base plan: house walls, doors, windows, fences, shrubs, tree trunks and leaf canopies, existing irrigation, spigots, pools, paving and paths, overhead and underground utility lines, drainage courses, property lines, easements and setbacks, and shadow patterns of neighboring buildings.

Once every significant detail is recorded on the base plan, the plan can be traced onto a clean sheet of paper. The newer version will be more precise and easier to read. Use the architect's scale to compute dimensions, triangles to check angles, and a template or compass to draw true circles.

Base Plan With Notes

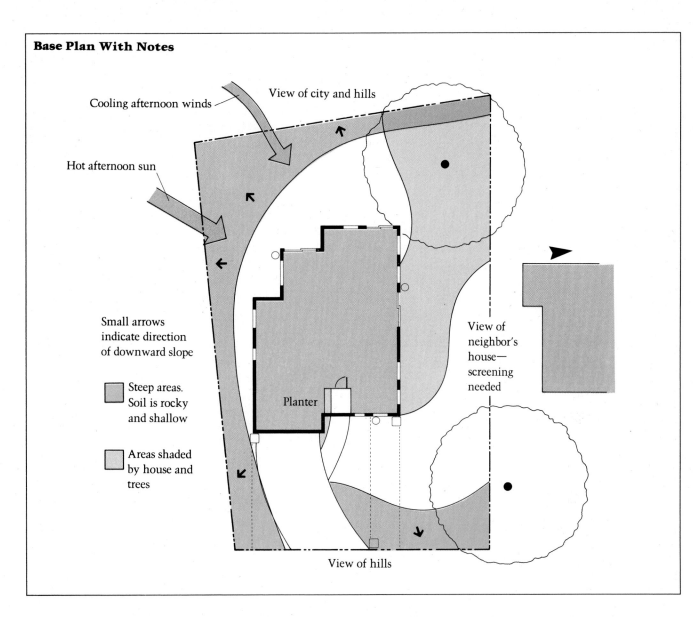

Cooling afternoon winds

View of city and hills

Hot afternoon sun

Small arrows
indicate direction
of downward slope

Steep areas.
Soil is rocky
and shallow

Areas shaded
by house and
trees

Planter

View of
neighbor's
house—
screening
needed

View of hills

Notes on the Base Plan

Now take this clean, accurate copy and return to the site. Cover it with an overlay of tracing paper, and record the following information: views (both good and bad), buildings and other objects, shadow patterns from large trees (patterns from deciduous trees will change as the trees lose and regrow leaves), sunny spots, direction of the prevailing wind, wind-free areas, areas where snow drifts or rain runoff collects, and access points and circulation routes. Note how well each feature works—or fails to work—in the garden.

Make a note of any trees or shrubs that will be removed, as well as those that will be saved. Are there any lawn areas, ground covers, large rocks, or other elements that will need to be removed in order to accommodate new ideas? If so, indicate these on the plan.

If a grade will be altered—by either removing it or decreasing it—mark it on the plan. Drainage problems can affect the intended use of a particular space. If water collects in an area where a patio or other activity space will be located, be sure to read the sections on drainage in the sixth chapter, "Installing Your Landscape," before planning a solution. Indicate on the base plan the areas that will need drainage and drainage systems. The location of retaining walls and their height, width, and slope (if any) should also be noted. Details for constructing walls can be found on pages 101 and 102.

Now is also the time to think about watering systems, because irrigation is a primary consideration in any garden. Plans for various types of irrigation systems are detailed on pages 89 to 99.

At this point the base plan may contain a confusing number of notations. For the sake of clarity, make a tracing of the basic lines of fixed forms, such as the house walls and the street curb, and work from them. But don't dispose of the marked base plan, because it will be helpful in the concept-drawing phase.

Seeing With Fresh Eyes

In spite of all the knowledge gained by making a base plan, put off the urge to hurry into construction, and take the time to develop a design. Look at the site as a first-time visitor would; don't let preconceptions limit the possibilities for your new design.

The best way to develop new ways of seeing the landscaping possibilities of a site is to become familiar with the design concepts discussed in the third chapter, "The Elements of Design." For example, what would the views to and from the areas you want to landscape be like at different elevations either above or below ground level? Can the house be connected to the garden with a deck, thus creating a better circulation pattern between them? How will a new deck or patio look from inside the house? From the street? Climb up a ladder to check out views from possible raised decks. Outline ground-level areas with water hoses or string to determine what they will look like when set off in various ways. In general, broaden the limits of the site as much as possible: The better you know the site, the more easily you will think of new ideas.

Design Checklist

Once the base plan has been completed and includes all the necessary notations, ask yourself specific questions, using this checklist as a guide. The purpose of this exercise is to ensure the soundness, appropriateness, and completeness of the plan. The checklist will help you clarify your needs, better understand the potentials and limitations of the site, and arrive at a workable design.

Uses of the Garden

☐ Which of the present uses of the garden are important to maintain, and which should be eliminated?
☐ What are the functions of the redesigned garden? Consider how the garden will incorporate the appropriate space and facilities for relaxation, entertaining, recreation for adults and for children, vegetable and cut-flower gardening and other hobbies, keeping pets, and other activities.
☐ Which of the planned uses will be a permanent part of the garden, and which are only temporary or are likely to change? For example, the landscape may include a children's play area, a vegetable garden, or a dog run. Consider from the outset future uses for areas with temporary features.

Characteristics of the Site and House

☐ Does the site have underground utility lines, water pipes, wiring, or television cables? Where are they?
☐ What aspects of the architectural style of the house do you want to extend to the landscape?
☐ What features of the existing landscape do you want to preserve or emphasize? Include elements such as plants and structures, as well as views.
☐ What are the unattractive features of the landscape? Detail those you want to remove, modify, or screen.

Elements of the New Garden Design

☐ Is there a particular landscape style you want to follow?
☐ Are there any design ideas from "Landscape Style" or "The Elements of Design" that you want to include?
☐ Should some areas be more private or more accessible?
☐ What outdoor rooms do you want to create in the new landscape? What are their purposes?
☐ Are there any special plants, structures, or other elements you want to add to the garden?
☐ What colors of foliage and flowers do you want?
☐ What sort of paving surfaces do you like?

Practical Considerations and Special Needs

☐ Are there easements, setbacks, zoning restrictions, building codes, or other considerations that may affect the plan?
☐ Will the plans affect the neighbors? If so, have you discussed the plans with them?
☐ What is the budget for the project? Can the project be staged to fit within the budget and still fulfill your long-term plans?
☐ Are the materials for the project readily available and affordable?
☐ How much time do you have to carry out planning, design, and installation?
☐ Do you have the necessary tools, skills, and patience to complete the project yourself?
☐ How long do you expect the garden to last before it needs another major remodeling?
☐ Will you have time to maintain the garden once it is installed?
☐ Are any members of the family allergic to specific plants or bee stings?
☐ Do you have a concern for conserving water?
☐ Do you want to attract birds or other wildlife?

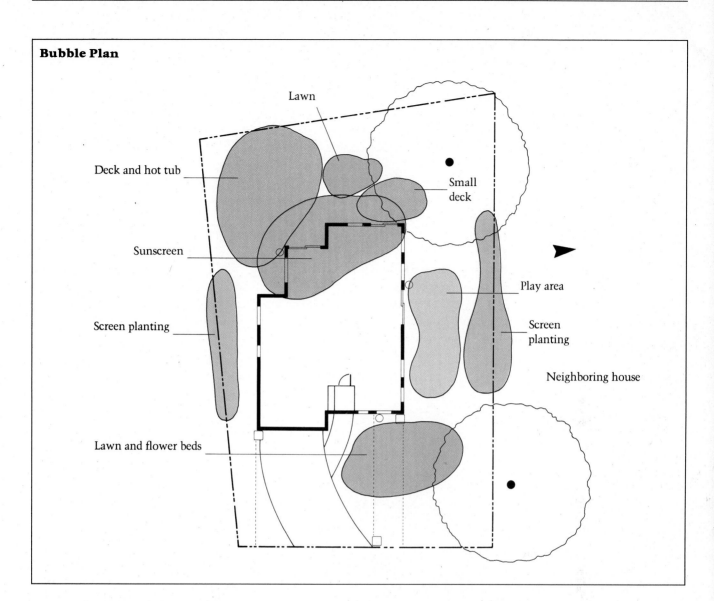

Bubble Plan

Lawn

Deck and hot tub

Small deck

Sunscreen

Play area

Screen planting

Screen planting

Neighboring house

Lawn and flower beds

FROM BUBBLE PLANS TO CONCEPT PLANS

Some people can visualize designs easily, but most people need time to find a solution to a design problem. For this purpose, a series of sketched plans done on tracing paper is as inexpensive as it is indispensable.

Bubble Plan

The bubble plan is a way of thinking on paper. When tracing paper is placed on top of the base plan, it is possible to experiment endlessly with design ideas. A bubble plan will keep you from thinking about details when you should be concentrating on general considerations. During the concept-plan and working-plan phases, the plan can be refined and actual components, materials, and dimensions can be selected.

Make quick circles or "bubbles" to represent the various spaces that will be created in the garden. The different sizes of the bubbles will indicate their respective uses and relative importance.

Keep in mind that these spaces are for activities—planting, eating, relaxing, and socializing. Think of the connections between these spaces, such as easy access from outdoor cooking area to kitchen, or from spa to bedroom or den. Be conscious of circulation—where people will need to walk, and areas that should not be busy thoroughfares. The effective use of any room may be diminished if it becomes simply a corridor from one place to another. Most of all, be aware of how well the bubble plans meet your particular needs.

The garden can be changed fundamentally, both in appearance and in circulation patterns, by altering its contours. Consider modifying the slope or terrain—for example, raising an area above ground with a deck, or leveling a hilly area for a patio. Consider also how the landscape will look from interior rooms, how existing garden elements can be incorporated, and the orientation of the spaces in relation to the sun angle, views, noise, and winds (as noted in the base plan).

Another way of determining spaces and their interrelationships is to make bubble shapes from cardboard or paper. The pieces can then be moved around on the base plan in order to try out different configurations. The final combination can be traced and put aside to reconsider later.

Once several agreeable combinations have been developed, go back over each and see whether it accomplishes the design goals. Finally, choose the one you like best. This will be the basis for the concept plan.

Concept Plan

After a bubble plan is developed, the concept plan will help to define how the spaces in the garden might actually look and what size each will be. For example, the area marked for play on the bubble plan perhaps should be a lawn twice as long as it is wide and separated from the eating area with a low wall or line of shrubs. The outdoor eating area might become a paving-stone patio connected by a path to the kitchen.

When determining the right size to make the spaces, use the size of the equivalent indoor room as a guide. For example, a space intended for outdoor dining and a barbecue can follow the dimensions of a good-sized kitchen and dining alcove as a starting point. But don't make outdoor spaces (for instance,

Concept Plan

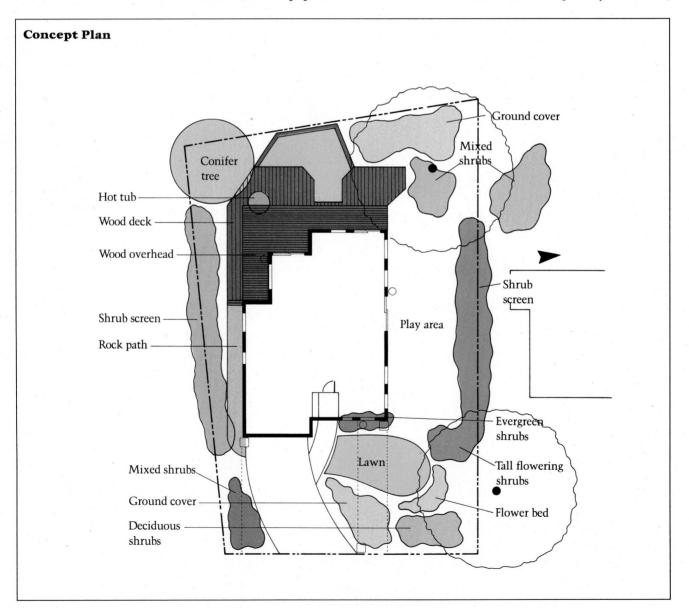

patios and decks) so large that they are uncomfortable and inconvenient.

If a deck or patio will be used primarily for entertaining, think of how much space it takes to entertain the same number of people indoors, and whether more space will be required outdoors. A sense of intimacy outdoors depends upon the size of the room in relation to its purpose and to human scale.

Detail sketches   These can help to visualize certain aspects of a concept plan. Detail or thumbnail sketches are usually very simple and focus on one specific aspect. A bird's-eye view is a sketch drawn from an angle above the site or object. Section drawings show a cross-section profile of an object or area. For example, a section of a deck would show the railing, the surface of the deck, and the joists, beams, posts, and footings. Section drawings are good for studying how walls, seating, decking, or any element with a vertical composition fits together in the design. Elevations also express vertical composition, but instead of showing a cutaway view, they present an object head-on, such as the front of a house.

Simple sketches of sections and elevations will help to formulate ideas and communicate them to other people. Many people who find it difficult to visualize a plan can understand a simple sketch. See the examples of each type of sketch below.

Before proceeding to the working drawing, estimate the costs of labor and materials called for in the concept plans. Guidelines for this are on page 76.

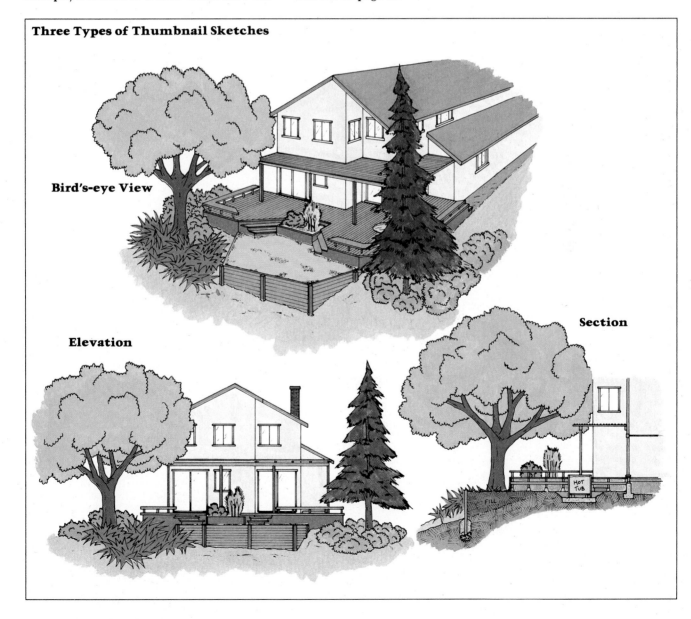

Three Types of Thumbnail Sketches

Bird's-eye View

Elevation

Section

Working Plan

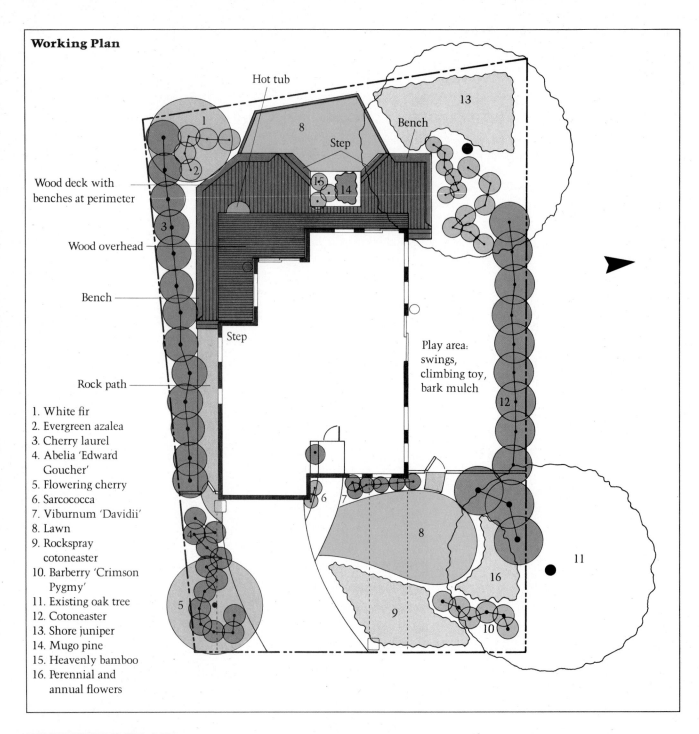

Hot tub

Bench

Wood deck with
benches at perimeter

Wood overhead

Bench

Rock path

Step

Step

Play area:
swings,
climbing toy,
bark mulch

1. White fir
2. Evergreen azalea
3. Cherry laurel
4. Abelia 'Edward
   Goucher'
5. Flowering cherry
6. Sarcococca
7. Viburnum 'Davidii'
8. Lawn
9. Rockspray
   cotoneaster
10. Barberry 'Crimson
    Pygmy'
11. Existing oak tree
12. Cotoneaster
13. Shore juniper
14. Mugo pine
15. Heavenly bamboo
16. Perennial and
    annual flowers

WORKING PLAN

A working plan is an accurate, scaled rendition of the final concept plan, so named because its information should enable the landscape to be built. The detail it contains depends on how much is needed to communicate to someone else, such as a contractor or city building inspector. A working plan indicates graphically what kind, what size, and how many of each item will be required to complete the project. It also shows how to put the materials together to make the landscape.

Once the three or four best ideas have been combined into the final concept plan, test it before beginning to draw the working plan by making several simple elevation sketches from different angles, and work through the plan again with a fresh overlay. Take the plan outside and walk around the spaces shown on paper to imagine the proposed design. Check to be sure that it includes everything. Access and circulation routes should be workable, and screening or view requirements should correspond to the notes made earlier. The plan

Plans for One-Story, Single Family Home

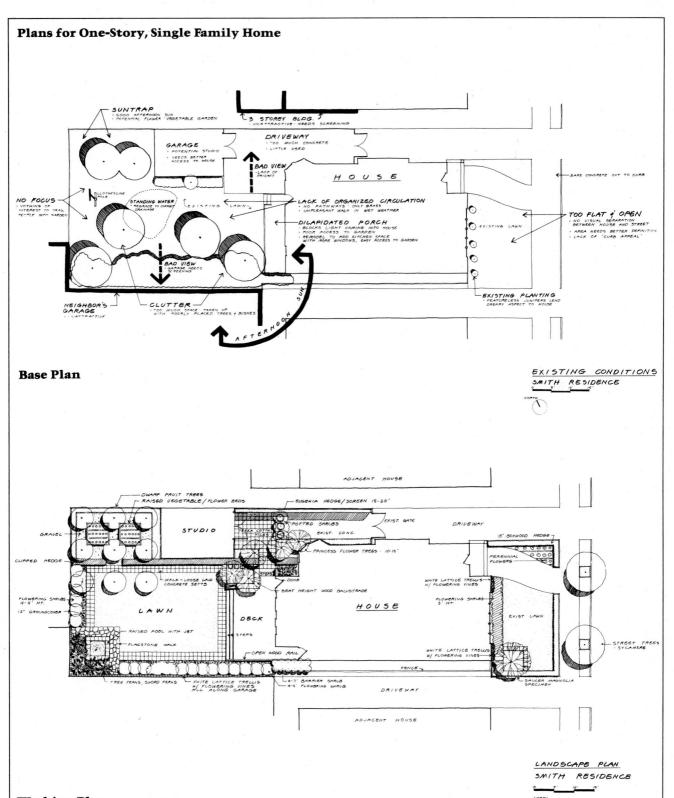

Base Plan

Working Plan

Although they could not afford to install all the features they wanted at once, the owners of this home designed future developments into their plan, including structural elements to build later. By varying the garden levels, using a variety of plant materials, and creating areas for specific purposes (a vegetable garden, a lawn, and a deck for relaxing), much has been done with limited space. Views of neighboring homes are blocked by plant screens, and a pool with a water jet provides visual appeal and muffles street noises.

should fit the time and budget necessary to execute it. Next, trace the concept plan neatly, and use the tracing as the basis for the working plan.

Add measurements to all the spaces on the working plan. Be exact and, wherever possible, use the standard sizes of available materials. For example, if fencing material comes in 4-, 6-, and 8-foot lengths, don't decide to make a 5½-foot fence; it will create extra work and expense, and waste material. Although this may mean choosing dimensions that are slightly different from those on the concept plan, it is better to make the changes at this stage than during installation.

When thinking about problems that might arise during construction, try to consider all possibilities. Make detail sketches and notes on the plan that show how potential problems will be solved. Sample details might include how to dig a hole for a particular tree, how deep it should be, and what it will be back-filled with; how a group of new trees will be staked in a windy location; or specific ideas for the construction of a retaining wall.

On the working plan, make notes of any detailed information that should be remembered, such as the color of paint or stain for a fence, plant names and sizes, or water requirements for a special tree. Much of this can be included in a plant schedule—a list of plants with quantities for each—placed either directly on the plan or on a second sheet.

When drawing the working plan, apply even pressure to the pencil to make a solid black line. Keep the lead sharp and remember to turn the pencil to ensure that the drawn lines are even in width. Lines that represent important, solid features should be bolder and darker than those for less significant items. For instance, steps and elevation differences should appear bolder than handrails. Indicate the eventual spread of trees by drawing circles. Also show what will be planted under the canopy of leaves. Remember to plant masses of the same type of plant for the greatest effect. Connect plants of the same type with light lines ending in an underlined notation of the plant name or mark with numbers.

If the plan is drawn on tracing paper, it can be made into a blueprint. Check the yellow pages of the local telephone book under blueprinters. Have five or six copies made at the same time; this usually costs no more than for one or two.

ESTIMATING COSTS

To get an idea of the cost of improving a landscape, find out what and how many of each item will be needed. Make a rough estimate based on the per-square-foot cost of the various materials before the concept plans are finished and a working drawing is made so that they can be modified if the estimate is dramatically over budget.

To make a really accurate cost estimate, however, it is necessary to have a complete working plan that spells out what and how many of each specific item is required. This book cannot provide accurate prices because of the regional differences in costs and the rapidly rising rates of most commodities; instead, check with local suppliers before figuring a final cost estimate. Be sure all basic costs are included, and compare the relative costs of different methods, materials, and strategies as the working plans are developed.

For a cost estimate, list all the materials needed from each different supplier. Put the plant, lumber, plumbing, and other materials on separate lists. Once these lists are complete—with specific materials, quantities required, sizes and dimensions, catalog numbers, and other information helpful in ordering—call suppliers to find out which offers the best deal. Remember that buying in quantity often brings prices down, and that purchasing from the original source of the supplies results in lower prices.

When picking up the materials, look for flaws in quality. Check plant material for form, root-bound problems, and general vigor. Examine lumber for defects. Before signing for deliveries, make sure the quantities delivered match the quantities ordered.

LEGAL CONSIDERATIONS

Obtaining the necessary city permits for construction plans can be an important part of making a landscape. If improvements will extend over the property line onto city land, or if the plans include a structure falling under the review of the building department, the working drawings should be checked by the proper authority.

Planting, paving, and other simple improvements usually are exempt from city review; however, some fences, irrigation, electrical work, almost all building structures, and most plumbing require a building permit and, in many cities, physical inspection of the finished project.

If you are unsure if a permit or other approval is needed, play it safe and check with the local building department about the work you plan to do. Remember that the building department also exists to prevent costly and possibly dangerous mistakes. Avoiding the inspection process may eliminate a fee and a bit of inconvenience, but it also may cause a lot of trouble if the code is ignored.

Most local planning agencies have zoning regulations that require setbacks, or borders to lot lines. In some areas, zoning often limits the percentage of the lot that can be covered with buildings or paving. Some localities even have tree ordinances to protect so-called heritage trees that are considered the rightful property of the entire community, even though they are growing on private land.

If the improvements will conflict with established zoning regulations, a variance can be requested. This exception to the regulations is given by the local appeal board when there are arguments that support it.

Variances are intended to provide a bit of flexibility to the hard-and-fast safety and quality standards of urban development. If a proposal is reasonable and does not interfere with a neighbor's interests, the local planning board will probably approve the request.

In most cases, at least two prints of the plans, clearly showing the intentions for the space, must be submitted to apply for a variance. Working plans are an excellent way to indicate the changes that will be made in the landscape. Check with the local building department for the established procedure.

Contractors and Contracts

If working plans are to be sent out for bids by contractors, make sure that the job description includes everything that must be done. Specify the quality of each material required; otherwise a contractor who wishes to submit the winning bid may use the least expensive materials suitable for the job. To prevent this, spell out the exact expectations on the plans

themselves, or write up separate specifications. The plans and specifications will become part of the contract documents, and they will clarify for both you and the contractor exactly what is to be done.

Most contractors will require a signed contract before beginning actual work. Read the entire contract and add any paragraphs necessary to protect your interests. Be sure that the contract requires the contractor to follow your plans and specifications. It is also wise to specify, in writing, that the work be finished by a certain date. A clause in the contract calling for a per-day penalty for late work will give the contractor an incentive to complete the project on time. In addition, a bonus can be offered for high-quality work completed ahead of schedule.

Most contracts require an initial deposit or advance. Make sure to indicate that a portion of the total fee is payable two to four weeks after the scheduled completion date. This requirement will help ensure that any final details will be completed relatively quickly.

Many states have legislation governing home improvements done by contractors. Most of these laws protect the consumer. Become familiar with them before starting a project.

Liens

Whenever outside people are hired to work on property, remember that there may be lien liabilities if the contractor (or the client) fails to be financially responsible. If a contractor hires subcontractors to carry out some of the work and then fails to pay them, they can make a claim against the property owner. For instance, a contractor may subcontract out a portion of the job, accept an initial deposit, and then go out of business. If the subcontractor was not paid for the work performed, the homeowner may be subject to a lien against the property, which must be paid off before the property is refinanced or sold. Avoid liens at all costs. The contractor should be paid in increments, so that there is enough money in reserve to cover the subcontracted work if the contractor does not.

Written assurance should be provided that workers' compensation and liability insurance are carried by every contractor. Otherwise, the property owner could be liable for huge settlements in the event of an accident.

Installing Your Landscape

If the design process has been thorough, installing the landscape should be a straightforward task. If you do the job yourself, you will have a lot of hard work, but watching the design come to life makes the effort worthwhile.

N ow that the landscape is designed, at last it is time to take a shovel and begin moving soil. But first, take a moment to shorten the installation process by carefully thinking out the schedule. This will spare you and your family from living with an unfinished garden for longer than is necessary.

The installation process is divided into 12 steps (see page 80). During the pauses between steps, you can appreciate a job well done and clean up piles of materials, open ditches, or unfinished construction that, if left untended, might be damaged or present a hazard.

Different steps take varying lengths of time. As a good rule of thumb, carefully estimate the time for a job, then double that estimate—a job always takes longer than anticipated.

The results of some of these steps may be disappointingly difficult to see—for instance, the yard will look just about the same after the sprinkler system and wiring for the outside lights have been installed as it did before. Remember, however, that some of these features are supposed to be invisible.

On the other hand, some aspects of a job seem to go very quickly. This is why construction is very satisfying—as soon as all or part of a construction project is finished, you can look at the new deck or gazebo with a feeling of accomplishment. Planting has the same magic; you feel satisfied when looking at a finished landscape with its plants and newly sodded lawn in place.

Rolled sod is ready to be installed.

The 12 Steps to Installing a Landscape

Not all of these steps will be necessary for each job, nor must they always be done in this order. However, by taking each into account in planning and carrying out the installation of a garden, you will avoid wasted time and extra effort.

1. Clean the site.
Clear site down to bare soil, leaving only those plants and features that will be included in the new landscape.

2. Make the rough grade.
Establish proper drainage slopes and make all major contour changes to conform with the landscape plan.

3. Install drainage system.
Dig and prepare all trenching for underground drain pipes, irrigation system, wiring for sprinkler system and outdoor lighting, and any other underground systems. Install drainage system.

4. Install irrigation system.
Install irrigation lines and any wiring in prepared trenches. Backfill and compact all drainage and irrigation trenches and re-establish rough grade.

5. Improve the soil.
Spread soil amendments and fertilizers, and rototill.

6. Construct hard-scape features.
Build and install all wood (fences, gates, decks), concrete (paths, retaining walls), masonry, and other constructed elements.

7. Install headers.

8. Contour to final grade.

9. Install large container plants.
Work from largest to smallest, planting all container plants over one gallon.

10. Plant ground covers, bedding plants, and lawn.

11. Clean up site.

12. Establish and care for plants.

Not all the steps are rewarding. Especially at the beginning of the project, be prepared for thinking that the work is going too slowly, that not enough is getting done. To alleviate these worries, take comfort in the thought that the foundation of the garden is being laid, and that whatever time and money are being spent will prevent headaches and make life easier for many years to come.

When each step is done carefully, attention is paid to details, and the best quality materials affordable are used, the garden will grow and ripen. Year by year, it will give pleasure, and it won't fall prey to the many ills that make gardening a chore instead of the immensely satisfying occupation it should be.

STEP 1: CLEAN THE SITE

When putting in the landscape, the first step is to clear the site. There are three categories of material to be cleared away: debris, weeds, and construction features.

Picking Up Debris
Picking up debris is a task that someone else, such as a local high school or college student, can be hired to do. Work with the assistant so that the job is completed according to plan.

A debris box, which can be rented from most garbage-collection departments, saves loading a truck and hauling its contents to the dump. For convenience, place the box as close as possible to the site being cleaned.

An owner-operated tractor-loader and dump truck can also be hired. The operator can make a quick, easy job of removing the debris, as well as rough grading and readying the site for tilling and soil preparation.

Weed Control
Weeds can create two troublesome problems, but planning will save a great deal of anguish later on. The first problem is removing growing weeds, such as Bermuda grass, quack grass, or other difficult perennial weeds. The second is killing weed seeds left in the soil.

Removing growing weeds If these weeds are cut off or tilled in, they will resprout at full strength. Bermuda grass, for example, has a root system often as deep as 3 feet or more, and sometimes one spraying with even the most powerful herbicide—such as glyphosate, which translocates from leaves to roots—will not kill all the roots. To ensure maximum effectiveness, water the area two days after spraying and continue to water periodically for four weeks; if any grass sprouts, spray again when it is in full leaf.

If weeds are actively growing at the time of removal, spray them with glyphosate herbicide, leave them for a week, and then remove. Even if they may not look dead, the herbicide has been translocated throughout the root system, which will soon die. Because it breaks down quickly in the soil, it won't poison future plantings.

Left: If removing Bermuda grass or other deep-rooted lawn grasses, kill them first with an herbicide to keep the grass from resprouting as a troublesome weed later.
Right: A rented debris receptacle reduces the work of cleaning the landscape site by saving you from multiple trips to the dump.

Renting Tools

Many useful hand and power tools can be rented from hardware stores or rental agencies. This list is representative of the tools available. Ask a local rental agency for a list showing available tools and prices. For larger equipment, such as tractors, be sure that delivery and pick-up are provided.

Aerator	Front end loader with scraper	Power dirt tamper
Axe	Gas chain saw	Power posthole digger
Backpack blower	Hand dirt tamper	Rebar bender
Builder's level	Hand leveler	Rebar cutter
Concrete finishing tools	Horizontal boring machine	Rototiller
Concrete mixer	Lawn edger	Scythe
Concrete saw	Lawn mower	Seed spreader
Concrete vibrator	Lawn roller	Sod cutter
Crowbar	Limb chipper	Steel post driver
Electric chain saw	Mattock	String weed trimmer
Electric dirt spade	Pick	Trencher
Electric hedge trimmer	Pole pruner	Weed mower
Electric jackhammer	Pole saw	Wheelbarrow
Fertilizer spreader	Posthole digger	Wide rake

If weeds are not actively growing, they can be taken out immediately by using a soil fumigant, sometimes called a soil sterilizer. This is a serious step, as fumigants kill everything in the soil and are difficult to use properly.

To avoid having to use fumigants or stronger herbicides, plan the weed-control operation. By removing existing weeds before they go to seed in the spring or summer, there will be far fewer seeds and weeds in the soil.

Removing weed seeds   If the yard has been wild or weedy for some time, the soil is probably laced with the seed of weeds. They can be ignored temporarily—which is easy to do, since they can't be seen—but later on the weeds that emerge will have to be pulled from the garden.

Here's one simple way to remove weed seeds: Schedule a pause of two weeks to a month in the landscaping before planting begins. During this break, keep the soil damp to encourage germination of weed seeds. When ready to begin planting (but before the new weeds go to seed), spray them with a contact herbicide (glyphosate) that does not leave a soil residue. Hoe the weeds or till them in, thereby stirring up the soil to bring new weed seeds to the surface where they will germinate and may be sprayed in the same way.

Solarization   This is another simple method for killing weeds and other unwanted seeds that may be present in the soil. After using a rotary tiller on the area to be planted, wet the soil thoroughly. Next, cover the area with a sheet of clear plastic. Stake all sides of the plastic, or weight the edges to prevent air circulation and loss of moisture. The plastic will concentrate the rays of the sun, heat the covered soil, and cause the trapped moisture to turn to steam. The combination of steam and heat acts to kill many weeds and weed seeds in the soil. With this method, the soil should be mostly weed-free and ready for planting in three to four weeks.

Removing Trees and Shrubs
If cut off at soil level, some vigorous trees and shrubs will sprout from the roots. Resprouting can be prevented by killing the plant with a brush-killer type of herbicide (triclopyr) before it begins to sprout. Either spray it on the foliage or make downward-slanting cuts into the bark and pour brush killer into those cuts. Whichever method is chosen, follow the directions on the label carefully.

If possible keep from having to remove stumps; stump grubbing is probably the hardest, slowest work in a landscape project. If the area does not need to be cultivated, the stump can be cut off just below ground level. Over the years it will rot, leaving a depression that can be filled in.

Decayed roots often result in mushrooms or toadstools growing in the lawn. Because there is no method or herbicide available to easily control mushrooms or "fairy rings," it is important to remove major roots that extend beneath lawn areas.

If the stump must be removed and it is large, consider hiring a tree service, which will bring in a stump grinder—a large machine that will reduce a stump to chips in just minutes. Rent a stump grinder if you prefer to do the job yourself.

Removing Lawns
If an area is being cleared of grass that can be used in another place, rent a sod cutter to cut the sod into strips of one width (12 to 18 inches is convenient), and lay them out on a flat surface in a shady location (a patio or driveway works well). If watered carefully, sod will stay healthy for weeks.

Sod that is not needed or is in too poor a condition to use will still have to be removed.

If the lawn to be removed is of a grass variety that becomes dormant in winter, be certain that it is dead before removing. This lawn appears dead but, in fact, it is just seasonally dormant.

If the particular grass in the yard becomes dormant and turns brown in the winter, first kill it with an herbicide containing glyphosate; otherwise the deep root systems of these grasses will resprout even after the sod has been removed.

STEP 2: MAKE THE ROUGH GRADE

Try to plan the project so that soil won't have to be purchased or dumped. If possible, shape the yard by moving soil around; to build up a a low spot, find a high spot from which to take the required soil.

Buying Soil

If soil must be purchased, match the texture of the existing soil. It's unnecessary to buy exactly the same soil. If the heavy clay soil presently in the garden drains slowly, buy a good-quality clay soil that drains well, or a compatible soil with high organic content. Resist the temptation to lighten the clay with a sandy loam. Soils of radically different textures can cause drainage problems if they aren't mixed perfectly; water does not move easily from one soil texture to the other.

Soil is sold by the cubic yard. The minimum load most suppliers will deliver without a surcharge is 5 yards. Quality varies from soil to soil, as with most products. Some dealers may sell soil for three times as much as others. The highest quality available may not be the one to buy, but avoid the lowest quality—it may cause problems later.

Obtain prices from a number of different suppliers; then investigate the most promising possibilities. Find the location of their stockpile, and drive out to see the soil before ordering. It's hard to refuse a delivery from a dump truck that is already backed into the yard.

Have the soil dumped as close as possible to where it will be spread, even if it means taking out a section of fence or filling in a ditch to gain access to the backyard. A good driver can spread the load to the requested depth with remarkable precision, saving later work.

If someone in the neighborhood is installing a swimming pool, arrange to have the soil dumped in your yard—free soil for you and a convenience for the neighbor. First be certain that the soil is suitable for the garden and

isn't contaminated with the seeds of noxious weeds or with debris.

Moving Soil

This is difficult and laborious work to attempt with only a shovel and wheelbarrow. Instead, consider using hired labor, or renting a tractor or an owner-operated tractor. Rental agencies carry a wide assortment of tractors in sizes appropriate for a homeowner. In addition to making the job faster and easier, they are fun to work.

Above: After the grass dies, remove it with a rented sod cutter. Below: This rented tractor speeds up the heavy work of moving soil. Tractors are available in a range of sizes, from this backyard model to full-sized construction tractors.

Measuring Soil Slope

In most cases, the grade change can be made by eye, without measuring. However, if a critical or extensive grade change needs to be made, there are several devices that can help.

For short distances, buy a line level, a small spirit level with a pair of hooks that suspend it from a horizontal line. Attach a piece of mason's line to the tops of two stakes (driven into the ground firmly enough so that all the slack can be pulled from the line), and hang the level at one end of the line. It will indicate whether the line is level or when the stakes are at the same height.

For more complex jobs or long distances, rent a builder's level. This instrument resembles a surveyor's transit, but is much simpler to use. Set the builder's level on its tripod in the center of the yard. Ideally, all the points to be measured should be seen from this location. Level the tripod and look through the telescope. A horizontal line on the lens will cross the view point that is level with the instrument.

Levels are used with a surveyor's rod or a tape measure. Have an assistant stand the rod on a reference point (the corner of a patio or sidewalk works well). Record the number intersected by the line when the the rod is sighted through the level. Take similar sightings on other key points in the landscape. In each case the distance above or below the first reading is the height above or below that reference point. A lower number means that the ground is higher. Mark the measured points with surveyor's stakes (available from a lumberyard). Mark the elevation on each stake as it is planted.

A third, less expensive alternative is to use a water level. This simple device is attached to a garden hose and is more accurate over a longer distance than a line level. It will also function around obstructions that block the view of builder's levels. Water levels are available at most hardware stores.

Wherever soil will be added to a garden, first drive in stakes so that their tops are at the level to which soil will be placed. These will serve as guides for the leveling process.

Before moving any large amounts of soil, strip off the topsoil (usually the top 6 to 12 inches) and pile it to one side to redistribute later on. Topsoil is valuable for plant growth,

so don't bury it. Stripping topsoil requires a great deal of work and space, especially if the area to be regraded is large.

The primary reason for rough-grading and leveling is to establish proper grading so water will flow away from buildings and off the property. A sufficient minimum slope is 2 percent—¼ inch per foot for water flowing across soil or lawn.

Above: A builder's level helps find the precise elevation of any point in the yard. Use it in the planning stages to determine the amount of fill needed, or to measure slopes. Use it again to level soil, make cuts, fill in low spots, or pitch a drain line. Below: One of the simplest tests for soil quality is to feel the soil. Soil that crumbles easily and evenly is best.

Judging Soil Quality

The best garden soil is soft, friable, and free of rocks and weed seeds; it also drains well.

A handful of good soil is dark colored and has the texture of cake crumbs. Its color and softness are due to the high humus content. A moist clod breaks easily into crumbs and is not sticky. There are few rocks; and those present are pebbles. The soil contains no debris, such as sticks or building material.

Testing for weed seeds   If you have time, the presence of weed seeds can be determined by germinating a sample of the soil. Spread the soil 1 inch deep in a nursery flat or on a cookie sheet. Keep soil moist and warm (70°–80° F) for two weeks. Weed seeds in the soil will have germinated by this time.

Testing drainage   The best way to judge drainage is to dig a hole and fill it with water. After water drains out, fill it again and measure how fast water level drops. Less than 1 inch per hour means that soil drains too slowly. If this test can't be done in the yard, take a soil sample and test it in a tin can, as illustrated below.

Judging soil texture   The following guidelines will help you analyze the texture of the soil. First, determine whether the soil is generally dry or moist. Next, compare the characteristics of the soil with those described below to judge what type of soil is in the garden.

If the Soil Is Dry

☐ Sandy soil forms a weak clod that shatters into powder when squeezed.

☐ Loamy soil forms a moderately strong clod that breaks, but does not shatter, in your hand.

☐ Clay soil forms a hard clod that cannot be broken easily with bare hands.

If the Soil Is Moist

☐ Sandy soil feels gritty; clods break at a touch.

☐ Loamy soil feels soft; clods break easily into soft crumbs.

☐ Clay soil feels very sticky; clods are plastic—they deform in shape but do not break.

Testing Drainage

Drop the can on a hard surface a few times to settle the soil. Measure drainage only after water is dripping freely from the bottom of the can.

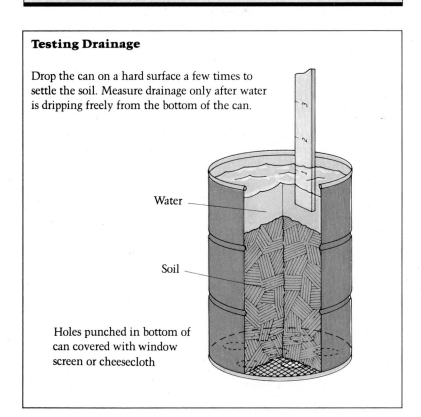

Water

Soil

Holes punched in bottom of can covered with window screen or cheesecloth

STEP 3: INSTALL DRAINAGE SYSTEM

The most important drainage provision is for surface drainage. If at all possible, slope the ground so that water will be carried away from the property. Ideally there should be 2 or 3 feet of fall for every 100 feet of horizontal land. The slightness of this slope moves water to a storm sewer or drainage ditch without letting it stand or puddle, and without creating erosion problems.

Be particularly careful not to shape the ground so that it will carry water toward the house. The land should slope away from the house for at least 4 feet at ¼ inch per foot on all sides (a 2 percent slope). In addition, make sure that the yard does not discharge water onto a neighbor's property, which, in some circumstances, may be a code violation. Check with the local building department.

Perforated Drain Lines

Drain lines are pipes with holes or slits in the undersides that carry away excess water. They are valuable for lowering a water table. If a hole dug in the yard slowly fills with water, the water table is too high for practical use in a garden. A drain line will lower the water table to the level of the line. Often it will help soil to drain more quickly after rain.

Because perforated drain pipe has holes in the lower portion to allow water to enter as soon as the water table rises to that level, be sure to position pipes with the holes facing down, not up. Some types of rigid pipe permit gluing of joints to ensure a watertight seal. Flexible drain pipe has slits all around the surface and snap fittings. Whichever type is used, be sure that the bottom of the trench is smooth, with a slope of 1 to 2 percent, and that the soil is tamped hard. Otherwise, the bottom of the trench might settle, and the pipe along with it, causing the sunken portion to clog with silt or bend and break.

If the soil drains slowly or water soaks in slowly because the soil is heavy clay or adobe, install surface drains or catch basins to carry away excess water.

Catch Basins

A catch basin is a vertical pipe in the ground into which water can run. The water in the catch basin is led to a drainage ditch or storm

Surface Drainage

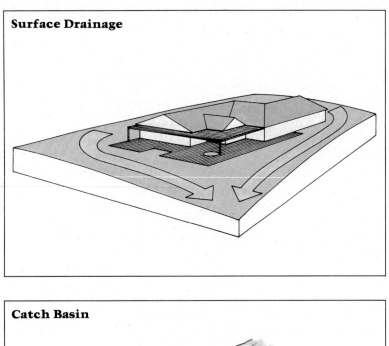

Catch Basin

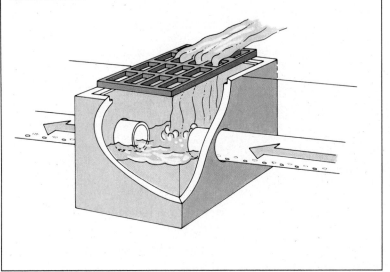

sewer by a pipe system resembling that of a drain line.

Catch basins can be ready-made or made by hand from concrete or treated wood. They are usually covered with a grate, but can be filled with rocks instead. Because catch basins accumulate silt, leaves, and other debris, be sure to clean them out regularly for proper functioning. Catch basins are useful in low spots where surface drainage will be ineffective, or where there is a particularly heavy flow of water to be channeled.

For sites where the flow of water is especially heavy, divide the area to be drained into a number of squares, each of which has been graded so that the perimeters are higher than the centers, which contain the catch basins. The ground should slope at ¼ inch per foot, or

2 percent. Connect all the catch basins into a solid drain-pipe system. All down spouts and perforated drain lines must be connected into this solid drain system as well. Solid drain systems are designed to discharge water into street gutters or other suitable drainage areas. If you have questions about drainage control, consult the local building department.

Installing an Underground Drain Line

To plan a drain line, first determine where the water will be taken once it leaves the line. Usually it will go into a storm sewer, street gutter, or drainage ditch. The point at which the water leaves the drain line is called the outfall. The elevation of the outfall determines the construction of the rest of the system. Since water moves through the line by gravity, there must be a fall from the top end to the bottom end of the line. There must be at least a 1-foot drop for every 100 feet of line, or ⅛ inch per foot, or the drain line will eventually fill up with silt and stop functioning. To find out how deep the line must be placed, start with the elevation of the outfall and measure backwards.

Plan to use a herringbone pattern, keeping the lines from 10 to 20 feet apart. If there is only one low area in the yard, a single line under it will probably be sufficient.

Start digging the ditch at the outfall, and work back into the yard. Maintain a steady upward slope from the outfall (minimum of a 1-foot rise per 100 feet of ditch, or ⅛ inch per foot) without dips, regardless of the contour of the soil. A simple level that may help is shown in the illustration at right. As you dig the ditch, drag this level behind you to measure an even 1 percent.

If the bottom of the ditch is rocky or broken, cover it with a 1-inch layer of sand or fine soil to make an even bed on which to lay the drain line.

Modern drain lines are made of a flexible, corrugated plastic hose. Light and simple to install, this hose will make all but the sharpest bends without the need of an angle joint. It comes in 3- and 4-inch diameters. The 4-inch hose offers the advantage of being less likely to clog if a piece of debris or a small animal gets stuck in it.

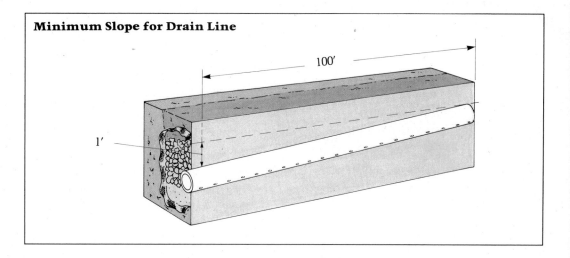

Minimum Slope for Drain Line

100'

1'

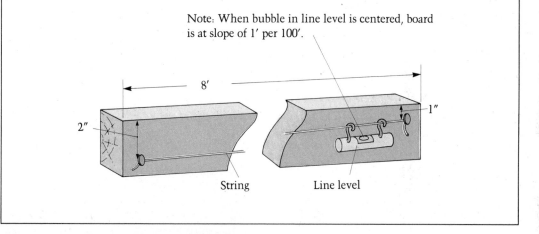

Homemade Tool for Measuring Drain Line Slope

Note: When bubble in line level is centered, board is at slope of 1' per 100'.

8'

2"

1"

String   Line level

Modern drain lines are lightweight, flexible, and simple to install. Use this type of line to lower a high water table, carry water away from low spots, and collect the runoff from a slope or from the house downspouts.

Other drain lines are made of rigid PVC or styrene pipe. Rigid pipe has the advantage that the joints can be glued, and the pipe can span short, low spots in the trench without bending. With rigid pipe there is also a better chance of routing out a blockage without tearing up the pipe.

Always lay perforated drain lines with the holes facing downward. This prevents soil from dropping into the line. It also lowers the water table to the bottom of the line, rather than to the level of the top, because water will rise into the line.

An effective drain system must be surrounded by an envelope of rock that will protect the lines, keep soil from entering them, and increase their capacity by conducting water. Use either smooth river-rock or crushed rock—the former drains faster, but the latter gives greater mechanical strength. Whichever is used, backfill the ditch with drain rock to a minimum depth of 4 inches over the line. In

Cross-section of a Drain Line

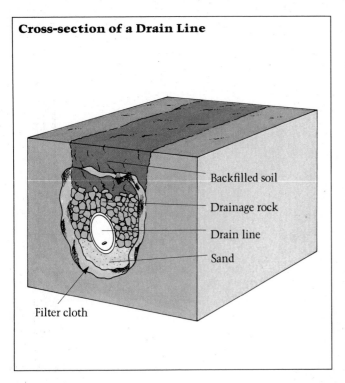

Backfilled soil

Drainage rock

Drain line

Sand

Filter cloth

Drain Line Designed to Catch Surface Runoff

Headers extend above ground level to hold rocks in place

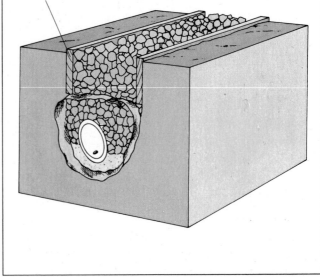

heavy soils backfill the trench with rock as high as possible so that water will have a minimum of soil to soak through. To prevent the envelope of rock from silting up, enclose it with soil filter cloth. Then install a clean-out—an access hole—at the highest point of the system. Place clean-outs every 100 feet or so in the drain line. Try to avoid using 90-degree bends, so that there is enough space to push a garden hose or sewer snake through the pipe for cleaning.

Now take the soil that was removed from the ditch and shovel it back in, backfilling the ditch to ground level. Before the ditch is full, run water into it to settle the soil; this will keep it from settling later on, after it has been planted over. This method can also be used to ensure that ditches dug for sprinkler systems or electric lines will settle before planting.

A variation on this drain line is to fill the ditch with drain rock up to the surface. This type of drain will allow surface water to enter the drain quickly, and will catch water that runs off a slope before it gets to the garden.

To keep soil out of the rock on the surface, place a couple of 2 by 6 headers on either side of the ditch, making sure that they extend 1 or 2 inches above ground level. Use an envelope of soil filter cloth, but be sure to cover the cloth with a final layer of gravel, since it will break down if exposed to direct sun.

STEP 4: INSTALL IRRIGATION SYSTEM

In an area where the yard must be watered more than a few times a year, a permanent irrigation system can save an enormous amount of time and work. There are several watering options: hand-watering with garden hoses connected to outdoor hose bibs; a permanent, underground sprinkler system; or a drip irrigation system. For best results, these watering options can be combined; for example, using a drip system for plants and ground covers, and watering lawn areas with an underground sprinkler system. Under no circumstances, however, should two different types of systems be combined on a single watering circuit (see page 96).

Garden Hoses

This is by far the least expensive option, requiring perhaps only a couple of hoses and some garden sprinklers. It can be a time- and labor-intensive process—depending on the location, it can take hours a week to move sprinklers from one spot to another.

Drip Irrigation Systems

A drip irrigation system consists of pipes, tubes, and hoses that can carry water to every shrub, tree, and ground cover area of the garden. Drip systems are generally less expensive to create than underground sprinkler systems, but have the disadvantage that they cannot be used to water lawns.

The system operates for hours each day, several times per week, applying gallons of water per hour (as compared with gallons per minute on a sprinkler system). Because the flow is slow and steady, water soaks deeply into the ground rather than wetting the surface and running off. Drip systems are especially useful in areas of heavy clay soil with poor drainage. Plants grow well when drip-irrigated because their roots receive a constant supply of water without ever being starved or flooded.

Emitters Many kinds of drip emitters are available. Among the more commonly used for trees and shrubs are emitters dripping any-

Opposite: An effective drain system must be surrounded by crushed rock to protect the line, prevent soil from entering, and increase the rate at which water percolates to the line.
Below right: A garden hose attached to a sprinkler is the least expensive, but most labor intensive, option for watering.

Drip Irrigation System

Antisiphon valve

Controller

Pressure gauge

Pressure reducer

Filter

Automatic valves

To emitters

where from 1 to 4 gallons per hour. Spray emitters, covering areas from 5 to 10 feet in diameter, are effective for beds of ground cover. Check with a local garden supplier, or obtain catalogs from sprinkler manufacturers to determine which types of emitters best suit the conditions of the site.

Installing the drip system A drip system can be a permanent installation of buried PVC pipe with emitters on risers, or it can consist of pop-up sprinklers similar to those of a standard sprinkler system. It can also be an above-ground system of hoses and tubes. The above-ground system, however, has certain limitations. It can be damaged by foot traffic, is susceptible to damage by rodents chewing through the lines, and, far more than a buried system, is vulnerable to freezing temperatures. Adequate protection from each of these hazards must be a part of an installation plan.

Since an emitter system operates under low pressure (5 to 25 pounds per square inch), the materials are inexpensive. But since the water must be carried to each plant, there is a lot of material to purchase. Up until fairly recently, drip systems had engineering difficulties. Now, however, the technology has improved so that a properly designed drip system can be as trouble-free and easy to use as a sprinkler system.

Sprinkler Systems

This type of system can cost hundreds or thousands of dollars to install, but over the years it will save many hundreds or thousands of hours of hand-watering. Automatic sprinkler systems usually take better care of plants, too—the timer never lets the garden go just one more day before watering and never floods it by forgetting to turn off the sprinklers. Therefore these systems conserve water and save money.

Planning the sprinkler system Since a complete sprinkler system represents a significant investment, there is a temptation to cut corners, locate heads too far apart, and use smaller valves. Resist this temptation. If you are unable to afford a complete system now, do a good job on part of the yard, leaving the connections for installing the rest of the system at a time when you can afford it. For

example, the necessary control wires for an automatic system can be installed at the same time as the pipes and valves. The control valves can be manually operated at first and later retrofitted with an automatic, electrically operated valve. This way money can be saved by not having to buy the electric controller and valve parts right away. Also, trenches will not have to be dug later when converting to an automatic system. Money well spent now means trouble saved later.

The following are general instructions for planning an automatic sprinkler system and are meant to present an overview. For more specific details, follow the manufacturer's instructions for the particular components you select. Before you begin, gather the pieces of information described below.

Service Line Size

Length of string	2 ¾"	3 ¼"	3 ½"	4"	4 ⅜"	5"
Size of copper-tubing service line	¾"	—	1"	—	1¼"	—
Size of galvanized-pipe service line	—	¾"	—	1"	—	1¼"
Size of Schedule 40 PVC service line	—	¾"	—	1"	—	1¼"

Chart courtesy of Rain Bird Manufacturing Corp., Inc.

Maximum Flow Rate

Water Meter	Service Line	Water Pressure (in pounds per square inch—PSI)					
		30	40	50	60	70	80
		Gallons Per Minute (GPM)*					
⅝"	¾"	3.5	7	10	11	13	—
	1"	4.5	9	12	13	15	—
¾"	¾"	5	8	11	14	16	16
	1"	7	11	15	17	19	19
	1¼"	9	13	17	19	21	21
1"	¾"	6	9	12	15	17	17
	1"	9	13	19	20	21	21
	1¼"	11	15	20	22	24	24

*Based on full flow rate (with no corrosion resistance) through a 75' service line. If your service line is galvanized, do a flow test since corrosion can limit the flow available. If the service line is PVC pipe, add 2 GPM to any of the above values.

Chart courtesy of Rain Bird Manufacturing Corp., Inc.

Finding the flow rate Call the local water company to find out your water pressure, or buy or borrow a pressure gauge from a sprinkler parts supplier. Attach the gauge to an outside faucet and open the valve; the gauge will read the water pressure in pounds per square inch. Take the reading at the time of day when the sprinkler system will be activated the most. The pressure can vary considerably with the time of day or even the day of the week, depending on the level of water use inside your home and how many neighbors are using water.

It is also necessary to know the size of the water meter (usually it is ⅝ inch, ¾ inch, or 1 inch). Read this information from the meter itself, or ask the water department.

The diameter of the service line—the line from the water meter to the house—is important to know. Wrap a piece of string around the pipe on the side of the house closest to the water meter, and measure the length of the string. Then see Service Line Size chart, page 90, to find out the pipe size.

Using this information, find the flow rate (see Maximum Flow Rate chart, page 90). The flow rate, in gallons per minute (GPM), is the amount of water available at the water meter to supply the house and run a sprinkler system. This information will be needed to specify sprinkler heads.

Get a catalog of sprinkler irrigation parts from an irrigation dealer. These catalogs contain specifications for sprinkler heads, valves, and other parts.

Designing the sprinkler system Working with the base plan of the landscape, design each element of the sprinkler system as you read about it in this book. Work with tracing paper overlays so that ideas can be tried and rejected without having to erase parts of the drawing. Each of the steps illustrated here can be drawn on a separate overlay; this way, the final plan will be clearer and easier to use.

It will be easier to show all the fittings and parts when beginning with a large-scale plan, as large as can conveniently fit on the drawing board. Keep the notes on the plan as small as possible to save space.

Don't be in a hurry to finish the design. Experiment with many ideas for designing the system. It will slowly evolve as different methods are tried, until you have an irrigation plan that will serve your purpose.

When the yard was measured for a landscape design, accuracy was important for showing relative proportions of various areas. The dimensions for planning the sprinkler system, however, must be accurate to within 1 foot or so. Sprinkler heads are designed with close coverage tolerances. If there is an error of 5 feet when the heads are installed, that part of the system may have to be redesigned.

The lower branches of trees can interfere with a spray pattern. Note the height of these branches and any other aerial obstacles on the plan. Also note the locations of curbs. Consider using pop-up sprinkler heads in vulnerable locations, since heads placed close to an

Above: A sprinkler design plan is just as important as the overall working plan for the garden. Below: Measurements used to develop the sprinkler design plan must be accurate to within about 1 foot.

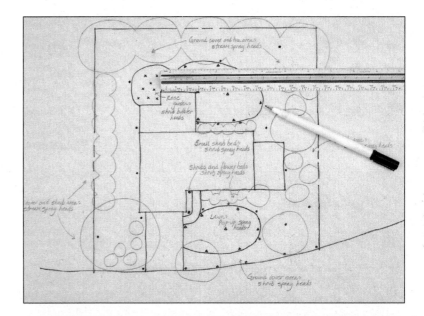

Irrigation Areas and Valve Locations

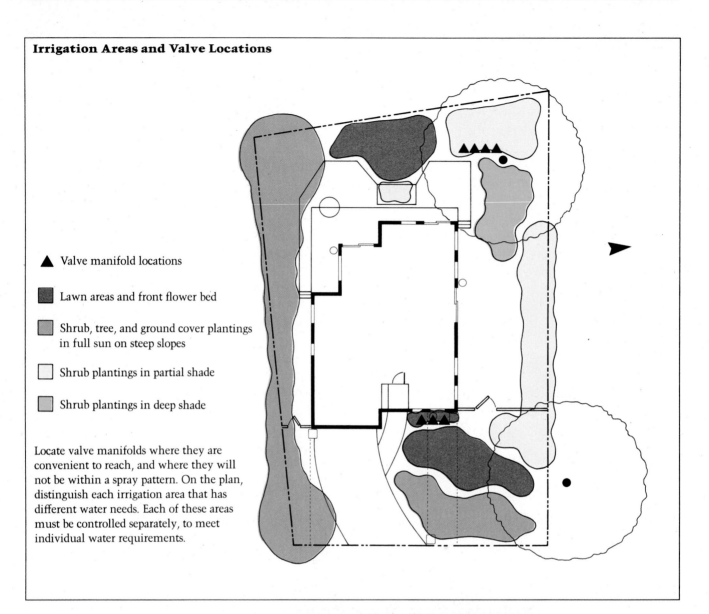

▲ Valve manifold locations

■ Lawn areas and front flower bed

■ Shrub, tree, and ground cover plantings in full sun on steep slopes

□ Shrub plantings in partial shade

▨ Shrub plantings in deep shade

Locate valve manifolds where they are convenient to reach, and where they will not be within a spray pattern. On the plan, distinguish each irrigation area that has different water needs. Each of these areas must be controlled separately, to meet individual water requirements.

uncurbed street or driveway will be constantly broken off. Pop-up heads—available in up to 12-inch heights—may also be used to rise above shrubs and ground covers.

Positioning the manifolds   A sprinkler system manifold is a group of valves that control the sprinkler system. The valves should be located in a convenient spot near an entrance to the house, where you can turn them on and off without getting wet.

If an automatic controller will be used to open and close valves, the valves can be positioned anywhere, but should be kept together because they will be much easier to maintain in the future.

Selecting sprinkler heads   Decide which sections of the yard will need to be watered

A sprinkler system is particularly helpful where irrigation is difficult—for example, where there is a steep slope or a complex planting plan.

Sprinkler Head Spray Patterns

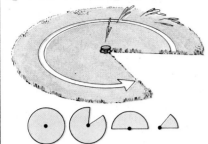

Rotating heads cover a large area. Mount them on risers for use over shrubbery. Available in pop-up models for large lawns.

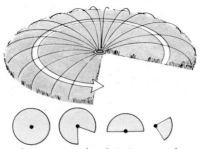

Stream spray heads irrigate gently and slowly. Use on steep banks to prevent erosion, or for heavy soil that puddles easily.

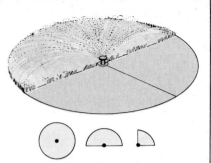

Lawn heads sit flush with lawn so that mowers clear them. Available in stationary and pop-up models.

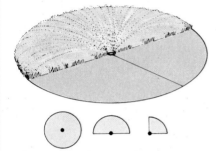

Flat spray heads are used under trees or shrubs to avoid wetting the leaves, or in windy locations where the low spray will not be easily blown.

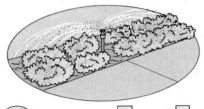

Shrub heads are on risers to clear shrubbery. As shrubs grow, install longer risers to keep the heads clear of foliage.

Bubblers let water run out onto the soil. Use with retaining wall or headers to contain water flow.

separately from other sections; each of these areas will be on a separate circuit. Always place areas of similar water needs on the same circuits. Lawns must be watered more frequently than shrubs, and sunny areas require more water than shady areas, and windy areas more water than sheltered areas.

Decide which areas should be kept dry—fences and walls will be bleached or discolored by water from sprinklers. Use the information in catalogs to choose heads whose spray patterns fit the plan. Plot the pattern covered by each head.

Select heads that use less than 60 percent of the available water pressure, and be sure heads on a single circuit do not exceed 75 percent of available flow.

Spacing sprinkler heads Space heads so that each one is just touched by the water thrown by adjacent heads. This 100 percent overlap is required to cover every area of the yard with the same amount of water, especially for areas of higher water demand such as lawn. In no case should there be an overlap of less than 50 percent.

When fitting odd corners, add an extra head rather than stretch the pattern—stretching the distance between heads is the mistake most commonly made in designing a sprinkler system. One small portion of the lawn may receive only half as much water as the rest of the lawn, and as a result, the entire lawn will have to be watered twice as long to keep that small portion green.

Once each head is chosen, write the catalog number of that head next to its location on the plan for reference.

Testing coverage An easy way to check coverage, once the system is operating, is to place flat-bottomed pans or dishes around the covered area, use the sprinklers for a while, then measure the depth of the water in each container. If the water depth is equal, there is equal coverage. If not, adjust the flow rates at each head accordingly.

Controllers A sprinkler system can be controlled manually or automatically. A fully automated system has a controller to turn the valves on and off.

Sprinkler Head Locations

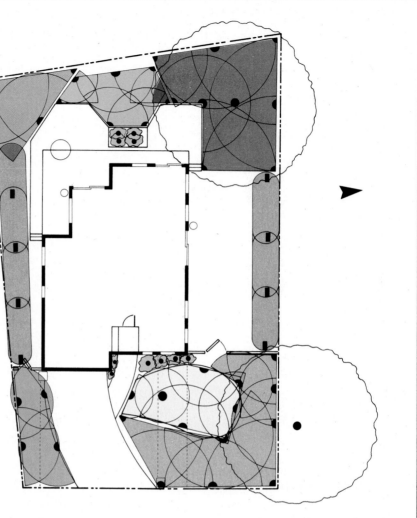

- ● Rotating heads on risers
- ● Pop-up rotating heads
- ● Stream spray heads
- ○ Flat spray heads
- ● Pop-up lawn heads
- ● Shrub heads
- ● Bubblers

Position sprinkler heads so every spot to be irrigated is covered by at least two heads. Space heads so water thrown from each touches the adjacent heads.

The controller will turn on each circuit at the time and on the days selected, and it will leave the circuit on for the length of time selected. For instance, the controller can water the garden in the early morning hours, as is done in most parks and golf courses.

There are two advantages to watering in the early morning. One is that few people are using water at this time, so there will be maximum pressure—an important consideration in some neighborhoods. The other advantage is that areas where people walk (such as paths or patios) don't have to be kept dry, since there is little foot traffic during these hours. For most gardens, the best time to water is between 3 and 6 a.m. Watering earlier can leave too much water on the plants and encourage disease. Ease of setting watering times is another good reason to consider installing an automatic system or retrofitting an established manual system.

Finished Sprinkler Plan

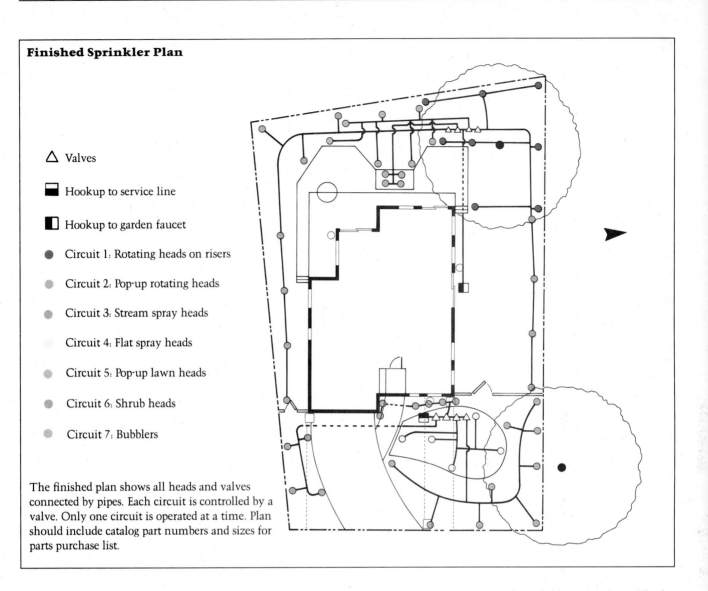

△ Valves

◨ Hookup to service line

◧ Hookup to garden faucet

● Circuit 1: Rotating heads on risers

● Circuit 2: Pop-up rotating heads

● Circuit 3: Stream spray heads

● Circuit 4: Flat spray heads

● Circuit 5: Pop-up lawn heads

● Circuit 6: Shrub heads

● Circuit 7: Bubblers

The finished plan shows all heads and valves connected by pipes. Each circuit is controlled by a valve. Only one circuit is operated at a time. Plan should include catalog part numbers and sizes for parts purchase list.

Opposite: To test whether the water coverage is even, place containers of the same size around the sprinkler head and measure the amount of water that accumulates in each.

Valves Some of the different types of valves used in sprinkler systems are described below.

Gate valves are inexpensive and simple to operate. A gate within the valve slides up and down to open or close the valve. Gate valves are used either as shut-off valves or are used in locations where watering is required only occasionally.

Antisiphon valves, also known as vacuum breakers, allow air to enter the highest point of an irrigation system to break any possible vacuum that could siphon water from the garden back into the main water supply. Antisiphon valves need to be placed so that they are higher than the level of the highest sprinkler head in the system.

Manual control valves are usually globe valves, the same type of valve that is used in faucets in the house. Globe valves shut off the flow of water by pressing a soft disk against a smooth valve seat. Manual control valves are used to control sprinkler circuits. All the valves for a front- or backyard are usually located in one place, in a valve manifold, for convenience. Sometimes antisiphon valves and manual control valves are combined in one valve body.

Remote-control valves are used with and governed by an automatic controller. They are usually electrically controlled by a solenoid mounted on the valve. Remote-control valves are often grouped together in a valve box placed in a convenient spot where they can be easily reached if repairs or adjustments are necessary.

Back-flow prevention Back-flow prevention is a vital part of any sprinkler system. Some type of device for preventing back-flow is required in most areas to protect against possible domestic water contamination in the event of a drop in the water pressure in the main service line. Check the local building codes for specific requirements. An anti-siphon valve is one such device (see description in the section on valves). Although they function well if properly installed, one drawback is that they must be installed at a higher level than the highest sprinkler head on the system. Also, they are not meant to withstand continuous pressure. Frequently, antisiphon valves are installed in combination with a manual or automatic control valve.

An alternative to the antisiphon valve is to install a pressure- type double-check back-flow prevention valve immediately downstream of the shut-off valve to the entire sprinkler system. This will protect the entire system from the dangers of back-flowing into the domestic water supply and will eliminate the need for an antisiphon valve. Be sure to check with an irrigation contractor or plumbing supply company to be sure the system is adequately protected against back-flow.

Designing the circuits   A circuit is a series of sprinkler heads controlled by a single valve and connected by pipes. Three rules govern the way circuits in a system should be designed.

□ **Zone coverage**   Areas with similar water needs should be covered by one circuit. Do not, for example, include shrubs or a rose bed and a lawn on the same circuit.

□ **Flow rate**   All the heads on a single circuit must use less than 75 percent of the available flow rate. The flow rate of each head is included in its catalog description. Add up the flow rates of all the heads on a circuit; the total must be less than 75 percent of the flow rate for your home. When the system is operated, only one circuit is turned on at a time.

□ **Sprinkler heads**   Only one type of head can be on a single circuit. For example, a bubbler cannot be put on a circuit with a rotating head; a rotating head cannot be put on a circuit with a lawn head. The sprinkler heads are connected with pipe lines, and these lines in turn are connected to the manifold.

Selecting valves and pipes   Check local plumbing codes to see whether there are any special restrictions on types or positioning of valves. Choose antisiphon valves for most locations. These prevent an accidental suction-

ing of water (containing fertilizer or pesticides) from the lawn back into the house supply. See the sections on antisiphon valves and back-flow prevention, page 95 to 96.

To find the valve and pipe size for each circuit (which depends on the combined flow rates of all the heads on that circuit) see Valve and Pipe Size (below). Write the catalog number of the valve on the plan.

The main feeder line from the house service line to the manifold should be the same size as the largest valve in the manifold. If the length of the feeder line is greater than 100 feet, specify a pipe one size larger than the largest valve—even if this makes the feeder line larger than the service line to which it connects. Next to each pipe length on the plan, write its size.

PVC Pipe Ratings

Polyvinyl chloride (PVC) pipe is manufactured under two different rating systems: schedule rating and class rating.

Schedule-rated pipe, which is rated like iron pipe, has walls that are uniform in thickness regardless of the diameter of the pipe.

Class-rated pipe has walls that become thicker as the diameter increases—this means that the pressure rating remains constant no matter what the diameter. The class rating indicates the strength of the pipe. Class 200 PVC pipe, for example, has a bursting strength of 200 pounds of pressure per square inch.

Schedule-rated pipe is stronger in the smaller diameters (under 1½ inches). Class-rated pipe is stronger in the larger diameters.

Pipe classes that are common in home sprinkler systems are class 315, class 200, class 160, and schedule 40. Class 200 is commonly used for lateral lines; class 160 is a less expensive alternative, but is more prone to damage.

Schedule 40 pipe is most often chosen for main lines and lines that bear pressure, and wherever the lines may be exposed to damage. Schedule 80 pipe is for locations where additional strength is required, such as for ½" sprinkler risers (for mounting heads) and for pipe-to-valve manifold connections.

Valve and Pipe Size

Maximum GPM* Flow	Use Valve Size	Use PVC Pipe Size	Use Polyethylene Pipe Size
0–9	¾″	¾″	¾″
10–13	¾″	¾″	1″
14–22	1″	1″	1¼″

*Gallons per minute
Chart courtesy of Rain Bird Manufacturing Corp., Inc.

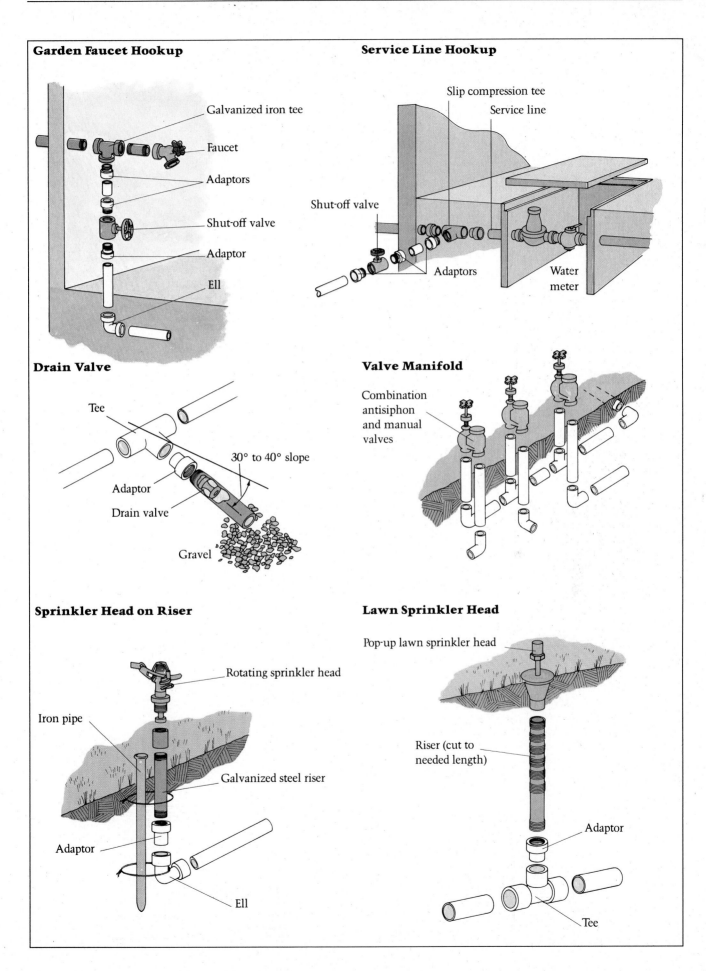

Garden Faucet Hookup

Galvanized iron tee

Faucet

Adaptors

Shut-off valve

Adaptor

Ell

Service Line Hookup

Slip compression tee

Service line

Shut-off valve

Adaptors

Water meter

Drain Valve

Tee

30° to 40° slope

Adaptor

Drain valve

Gravel

Valve Manifold

Combination antisiphon and manual valves

Sprinkler Head on Riser

Rotating sprinkler head

Iron pipe

Galvanized steel riser

Adaptor

Ell

Lawn Sprinkler Head

Pop-up lawn sprinkler head

Riser (cut to needed length)

Adaptor

Tee

Listing fittings Using detail drawings of manifolds and heads (see pages 93 and 97), write the size and name of each on the plan.

Locating the controller When using a controller, choose a proper location. For a non-weatherproof controller, select a location such as the garage; for a weatherproof controller, an outside wall of the house. In either case, try to locate the controller close to a 110-volt electrical source, where it will be easy to route all of the low-voltage valve wires.

Planning and installing automatic valves An automatic valve system operates from the low-voltage transformer in the controller. Wires will have to be run from the controller to the valves. First, connect a common wire, usually white, from the controller to each valve, leaving a 3-foot loop in each wire. Next run a separate wire of any color from the controller to each valve. Both the first and second wires must have 14-gauge, heavy-wall insulation that permits burial in the ground.

Where possible, try to route these wires in the same trench as the main water line to the valve in order to save additional trenching. The trench will need to be at least 1 foot deep; check with the local building department to see whether there are code requirements for low-voltage, direct-burial wire. All wire connections at valves must be made with waterproof connectors, several types of which are available.

Making a parts list On a separate piece of paper, list the valves, heads, fittings, and pipes that will be needed. As each piece is recorded on the list, circle its name on the plan so that it won't be counted again.

List the automatic controller, several small cans of PVC cement (½ pint), and a hacksaw or PVC cutter. Now the cost of the system can be determined and the parts can be bought.

Installing the sprinkler system Buy the necessary parts and gather the tools. The line from the house service line to the valves holds pressure; it is a live line. In this section of the line, heavier pipe and fittings are used, and building codes are more strict. You may wish to hire a plumber or irrigation contractor to install this portion of the system.

To install the manifold, first turn off the water to the house. Cut a 1¼-inch section from the service pipe and install a slip compression tee (you don't have to thread the cut pipe ends). Install a length of pipe and a shut-off valve in a valve box. If PVC fittings are used, the house water must be turned off for 24 hours for the PVC cement to set fully. Once it has set, the water can be turned back on. To avoid interrupting the water supply to the house, use metal fittings from the service line to the shut-off valve instead. Check with an irrigation or plumbing supplier for details on the types of metal pipe and fittings to use. PVC pipe exposed to the sun will begin to deteriorate over time, so use PVC pipe that is ultraviolet resistant.

Next, run lines from the valve box to the manifold locations and install the manifolds. The illustrations may look complicated, but if you start from the upstream end and add just one piece at a time, the process will be easier.

Now close the valves, open the shut-off valve, and test the manifold for leaks.

Installing the controller If using a controller, install it according to the manufacturer's

Parts List for Sprinkler System

Item	Quantity	Catalog Number	Description	Cost
Valves	1		1″ gate valve	
	1		1¼″ gate valve	
	6	ASV 200 A	¾″ manual antisiphon angle valve	
	1	ASV 200 B	1″ manual antisiphon angle valve	
Heads	5	P1500Q	¼ circle pop-up brass lawn head	
	5	P1500H	½ circle pop-up brass lawn head	
	1	P1500F	Full circle pop-up brass lawn head	
	1	SS2800Q	¼ circle stream spray shrub head	
	2	S1200ES	End strip shrub spray head	
	2	B1250	Shrub bubbler head	
Riser	12		½″ x 6″ cut-off risers (lawn heads)	
	22		½″ x 8″ schedule 80 PVC risers	
	34		½″ x 4″ flex risers	
	34		½″ schedule 80 PVC threaded couplings	
Pipe	60′		1¼″ schedule 40 PVC pipe	
	50′		1″ class 200 PVC pipe	
	380′		¾″ class 200 PVC pipe	
	220′		½″ class 200 PVC pipe	

This is a partial sample list of parts for a sprinkler system. Use this as a general guide to make a list for your system.

instructions, and lay the connecting wire to the valves. Most controllers run on a voltage that is low enough (24 volts) so that the wire can be buried without a conduit.

Laying out the system   Drive a stake into the ground at the location of each sprinkler head. Then use agricultural lime to draw lines on the ground where the pipes will be laid.

Digging the trenches   Trenches can be dug by hand or with a rented power trencher. If pipe will be laid through an existing lawn, cut the sod and put it aside; replace it when installation is completed.

Make the ditches at least 12 inches deep or, if they will be tilled over, at least 16 inches deep. In an area where the ground freezes, pipes do not have to be laid beneath the frost line; however, drain valves should be installed so that pressure can be released when the water in the pipe freezes (see page 97).

Power trenchers may be rented and are useful for digging straight, level trenches. A small, electric jackhammer can also be rented, and is very helpful for loosening packed clay soil.

Take advantage of the trenches to lay outdoor wiring, whether it will be installed immediately or in the future. See Ortho's book *How to Design & Install Outdoor Lighting.*

If pipe must be laid under walks, the easiest method is to dig the trench on both sides of the walk. Cap both ends of a piece of galvanized pipe long enough to span the length of the walk and with a diameter larger than the PVC pipe to be laid, and drive it under the walk with a sledgehammer. Insert the PVC piping into the galvanized pipe and draw it through the hole.

A second method is called jetting. Connect a small hose nozzle to a garden hose or piece of pipe. Turn on the water and use the jet to make a trench under the concrete.

Asphalt tends to collapse when trenches are run under it. The asphalt may need to be removed beforehand and later replaced over the backfilled trench.

Assembling the system   Tie the risers to the stakes that were driven at the locations of the sprinkler heads. Work backward to the manifold, assembling the pipe and fittings (leave the heads off). When all the parts have

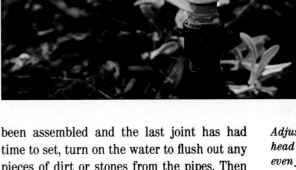

Adjust the sprinkler head to obtain an even flow and proper coverage.

been assembled and the last joint has had time to set, turn on the water to flush out any pieces of dirt or stones from the pipes. Then attach the heads.

Testing the system   Turn on each circuit, one by one; inspect the pattern carefully to make sure that every part of the ground is getting adequate coverage. At this point it is easy to add heads where they are needed. Try adjusting the amount of water spraying from each head and the radius of the coverage by turning the screw in the top of the sprinkler head. Other types of heads have other means of adjustment. Nozzles can also be changed in order to increase or decrease the radius. If a system makes too fine a spray (a fog), the valve should be turned down to reduce the pressure, being careful, however, not to reduce coverage.

Backfilling   Once the sprinkler system operates as specified by the design and is free of leaks, fill the trenches with the soil that was removed earlier. Stop just short of the top, remove the heads again, and slowly run water through all the circuits, or flood the trenches with a garden hose—the water will help settle the backfilled soil more completely, which will prevent settling and low spots later on. Replace the heads, finish filling the trench, and clean up the area.

STEP 5: IMPROVE THE SOIL

How much the soil needs to be improved depends on the condition it was in when the landscaping project began. If it was growing a healthy garden—or even a healthy weed crop—and water did not puddle up, the soil may not need much work.

Organic Matter

Organic matter, one of the best things that can be added to a garden, will improve almost any soil. It increases the capacity of the soil to absorb water and nutrients; it separates soil particles by opening and loosening the soil; and, as it breaks down into humus, it forms gluelike materials that adhere soil particles together into little crumbs, making the soil soft and friable (easily crushed or crumbled).

Most organic materials are beneficial to the soil. Wood by-products such as sawdust and composted bark are widely available; so are ground corncobs and peat moss. Other materials—including the farmer's standby, manure—may be available for the hauling. A home compost pile provides a continuing source of organic material.

Spread the organic matter on the surface of the soil between 1 and 2 inches deep. It is better to add a few inches each year than to add too much at once. The effects of a single addition of organic matter can last for years. However, in hot, dry climates, organic matter is used up very quickly. In an area where this is the case, consult a local nursery or agricultural extension office.

If the organic matter does not already contain a nitrogen supplement, consider adding ammonium sulfate or its equivalent. This will prevent the organic matter from tying up the available nitrogen in the soil as it decomposes.

Gypsum

If the garden has a very sticky clay soil that drains slowly, gypsum might help to improve its structure. Try mixing some into the soil in a small area at a rate of about 5 pounds per 100 square feet. Check improvement by performing the drainage test on page 85.

Lime

In many regions of the United States, including most areas east of the Mississippi River, the soil will probably benefit from the addition

Balancing Soil pH With Limestone

*Pounds of limestone per 100 square feet

Current pH	Sandy Loam	Loam	Clay Loam
4.0	11½	16	23
4.5	9½	13½	19½
5.0	8	10½	15
5.5	6	8	10½
6.0	3	4	5½

*Pounds of limestone denote quantities required to bring soil to a pH of 6.5. Hydrated lime is most commonly used as it obtains a more rapid reaction. Use three fourths as much as is recommended for limestone.

of lime. A soil analysis will reveal how much lime to use. If a soil analysis is unavailable, ask at a local nursery whether the soil needs lime. Refer to the chart above as a rough guide for the quantity of lime to use.

Fertilizers

Almost all soils benefit from the addition of fertilizer. Apply 20 pounds per 1,000 square feet of a balanced, general-purpose fertilizer.

Tilling

After these materials have been spread evenly over the ground, the next step is to till them into the soil. Tilling is most easily accomplished with a rotary tiller. Rent the largest one that can be operated easily and safely. Light rotary tillers are sufficient for soft soil that has been recently tilled. It is necessary to till only the areas where lawn and bedding plants will be located.

Most rotary tillers stir the soil to a depth of about 6 inches. It is important to reach this deep. If the soil is hard, there are a number of ways to till it deeply.

First, make sure the soil is sufficiently moist. If it hasn't rained recently, water the soil thoroughly, then wait a few days to let the soil drain before tilling. When a clod crumbles in your hand instead of deforming, the soil is ready to work.

Second, go over the soil with the rotary tiller a number of times. Each time, the soil will be tilled a little deeper.

Third, if all else fails, hire a contractor or an owner-operator to till the soil with a tractor-mounted tiller.

STEP 6: CONSTRUCT HARD-SCAPE FEATURES

By now, the yard has been shaped just the way you want it. It is time to add constructed features to the landscape.

As the heavy lumber trucks or concrete mixers make their deliveries into the yard, remember that there is a drain line under the surface. This line will withstand some pressure, but not as much as a full concrete truck will exert, so direct traffic attentively.

The subject of garden construction is a vast one. For detailed instructions on a wide variety of garden projects, see Ortho's book *Garden Construction*. This book discusses just two aspects of garden construction: hard-scape—that is, constructed—elements such as walls, walkways, and retaining walls; and irrigation systems.

Retaining Walls

You can build low retaining walls (under 3 feet) yourself, using a variety of methods; but since retaining walls over 3 feet must hold back a great deal of weight, it might be best to hire a contractor. In most areas, building codes apply to retaining walls over 3 feet.

Remember that soil has a tendency to flow downhill and, therefore, will press against the back of a retaining wall. Since the water in the soil causes it to flow, the water needs to be drained from the soil being retained. To do this, weep holes can be made every few feet near the bottom of the wall, or perforated drain pipe can be laid horizontally behind the wall so that the pipe will catch and carry away water. See the discussion on installing drainage systems, pages 85 to 88.

Dry-laid rock Rock or broken pieces of sidewalk laid against a bank will keep the face of the bank from eroding. This method works well for a low wall. Slope the bank a minimum of 2 inches for each foot of height, and lay the stones that face it at an angle into the bank, so that the bank supports their weight. Rock retaining walls are appealing in a natural or informal landscape. Plant succulents or rock plants in the crevices to further soften the effect of the wall.

Wood walls Wood, the most common material for retaining walls, makes a wall that

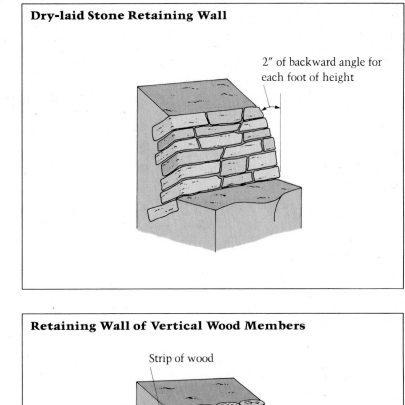

Dry-laid Stone Retaining Wall

2″ of backward angle for each foot of height

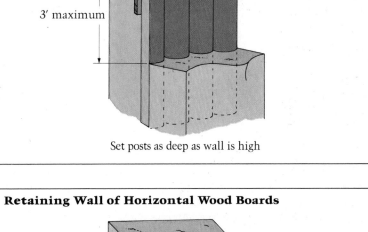

Retaining Wall of Vertical Wood Members

Strip of wood

3′ maximum

Set posts as deep as wall is high

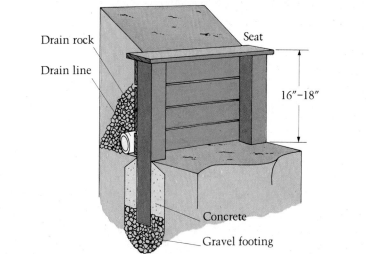

Retaining Wall of Horizontal Wood Boards

Drain rock

Drain line

Seat

16″–18″

Concrete

Gravel footing

lends itself to both formal and informal designs. If the wall is 16 to 18 inches high, a cap built on top can double as a garden seat.

Many types of wood are suitable for wall construction. The most durable is wood that has been pressure-treated for contact with the ground. Any wood that touches soil or concrete will decay over time. Although some woods naturally resist decay longer than others—for example, redwood—an approved wood preservative can be applied to ensure longer utility of the wood. Consult the staff of a local lumberyard for recommendations.

Vertical wood members   Sections of treated logs or railroad ties adapt well to curves in a landscape. Be sure to anchor them deep in the ground to keep them from leaning out. A good guideline is to put as much wood below ground as there is above, but not to exceed 3 feet above or below the soil. For added strength, set the wood members in a trench and pour concrete around them. Connect them at the upper back sides with a continuous piece of 2 by 4 or 2 by 6 pressure-treated wood. For curved sections of wall, double-laminated, continuous pieces of 1 by 4 or 1 by 6 wood works well. The wall may be capped with 2 by 10 or 2 by 12 pressure-treated or rot-resistant boards to make a low bench.

Walks

The simplest walk to install is one made of stepping-stones. A wide variety of materials are available, ranging from masonry stones to log rounds or railroad ties.

At the opposite extreme is a solid walk of poured concrete, or brick or stone set in concrete. To make this type of walk, see Ortho's book *Garden Construction*.

A third method of constructing paths is to use a loose material mix, such as gravel, bark, or wood chips. Like most loose materials they shift underfoot, making walking difficult, and rain tends to erode them.

In most areas, a soft rock mixture, such as decomposed granite, shale, or bluestone, can be purchased. In hardness these materials are about midway between gravel and soil. They pack into a firm surface such as soil, but they do not become muddy or support weed growth. They do, however, erode if water is allowed to run across the path.

Use strong headers on each side of the path, and place headers across the path as steps. Excavate to a depth of 2 to 4 inches, then spread the rock mixture in 1-inch-deep layers, wetting and rolling or tamping it firmly between layers. Crown the surface slightly so that it will shed water. The path will pack down and become harder with foot traffic. To maintain the path, level it occasionally with the back of a rake and re-compact. Compacting is best done with a rented vibrator plate, which creates a firm, level surface.

For any of these types of walks, consider using a weed-prevention fabric or black plastic beneath the surface. A variety of available fabrics will avoid the damage caused by weeds poking through the path.

Paths of decomposed granite offer many of the benefits of masonry paths without the cost and effort of installation. Build the path in 1-inch layers, wetting and rolling each layer as it is laid.

STEP 7: INSTALL HEADERS

Headers are wood, steel, masonry, or plastic edges around lawns or planting beds. They give a crisp, professional look to a garden and facilitate maintenance.

Masonry Headers

Brick makes attractive and semipermanent or permanent lawn edging if properly installed. Place bricks on sand or mortar; for permanence, mortar them to concrete footings. Concrete mow bands or edgings are relatively easy to install and can be finished to match the surface appearance of other concrete features on the premises. Concrete can be poured between bender-board forms to make curves. Pour concrete pads, 6 inches wider than the header, under either brick or concrete headers. See Ortho's book *Garden Construction* for details on concrete and brick work.

Wood Headers

Use only the heartwood of redwood, cedar, or cypress. Other woods will rot in a few years.

For the greatest strength, make headers of 2 by 4 material nailed to 2 by 3 or 1 by 2 stakes that are at least 1 foot long. Dig a trench, lay the headers in it, and stake them in place every 4 to 6 feet. Place the stakes on alternate sides of the header. Drive the stakes into the ground until they are flush with the header. Then place a block of hardwood atop each stake and continue driving it in until it is 1 inch below the top of the header. An alternate method is to cut the stake off 1 inch below the top of the header. This makes for a more finished look and does not interfere with the use of a lawn edger on the lawn side of the header.

Bender Board

Bender board, available in many lumberyards, is made of strips of wood about ⅜ inch thick and 4 or 6 inches wide. It is used to make curved concrete forms as well as curved headers. For best results, laminate two or three bender boards together as shown in the photograph on page 104.

Choose bender board made of heartwood, not sapwood, if the headers are intended to last for years. Sapwood, even of redwood or cedar, rots quickly in soil. The bender board should be uniform in thickness and flexible enough to form tight curves without breaking.

Right: To add gentle curves and bold lines to the landscape, use bender board. These flexible wood strips can be made into headers, as shown in this photograph, or used as concrete forms and mowing strips. Below: After the bender boards are in place, drive stakes every 3 feet, at all the joints, and on both sides of the bender boards at the ends. Holding a hammer head behind the board for support, nail each stake to the board.

Laying Out Curves

Here are three methods of laying out a curve in the landscape.

1. Draw a line with a stick. This method works well for ground that is soft and even-textured. The line, however, scuffs away easily.

2. Draw a line with lime. Holding a bucket of agricultural lime in your left hand, dribble the lime with your right hand. This line is almost scuffproof, but if it needs to be changed, you can correct it with a rake. This is a good way to experiment with proportions in the planning stages; a whole landscape can be drawn on the ground.

3. Lay down a hose. A garden hose makes an excellent line. It can be easily manipulated. When the position is correct, draw a line with lime over the hose.

To install it, dig a trench and pound in 1 by 2 stakes to hold the bender board in place temporarily. Wet the bender board for greater flexibility. Once it is in the correct position, drive in permanent stakes, as needed to hold boards in place. Locate stakes every 3 feet (closer on curves), at every joint, and on either side of the board at the ends. Drive the tops of the stakes 1 inch or so below the top of the board, as descibed for wood headers.

Hammer in enough nails to secure the stakes to the board, then place another board behind it and, for maximum strength, a third board. Stagger the joints and place new stakes at each joint. Nail all boards to the stakes with 8-penny galvanized nails.

Top-nail the bender boards together every 6 inches between stakes to keep them from spreading with age. Holding the head of a sledgehammer behind the boards, drive a nail through all three boards at a 45-degree angle, as shown in the photograph at right. When the nail hits the hammer head, it will turn and clinch itself into the wood.

Bender board is increasingly common, but may not be available in some areas. Check with a local garden supply store or lumberyard—if it is not in stock, someone might be able to make the boards on request.

Plastic Headers

Flexible plastic headers are a more recent alternative, especially for lawn edging. They are easy to install, will not rot, generally wear well, and are less expensive than most other types of headers.

Aluminum Headers

Another option, also becoming more readily available, is aluminum headers. These are offered in a variety of thicknesses and lengths. Avoid using the inexpensive aluminum edging that is often packaged in rolls—it is generally weaker and will deteriorate more rapidly than other edging.

STEP 8: CONTOUR TO FINAL GRADE

Once all of the underground improvements (drainage, irrigation, and wiring) and the headers have been installed, it's time to finish off the surface of the soil. In all but the lawn areas, a final raking will suffice. Use the headers as elevation guides. If the soil hasn't yet been settled by rainfall or irrigation, leave it about 1 inch higher than the headers to compensate for later settling. Be sure that the final grade will permit water to run off, not puddle. Most plants do poorly in soil that is saturated with water.

For areas on which lawn will be installed, a finer touch is needed. Use a wooden or aluminum leveling rake with an extrawide head and long handle to cull any rocks or clods larger than about ½ inch from the top 2 inches of soil. Level the ground even with headers, walks, and patios if the lawn will be seeded, or level it ¾ inch below the top of the headers if sod will be laid. Crown the soil slightly in the center to allow for effective drainage and possible future settling, especially if the soil has not yet been settled by rainfall.

Now wet down the lawn area, roll it with a lawn roller, and level it again. Repeat this process until low spots are eliminated.

STEP 9: INSTALL LARGE CONTAINER PLANTS

If the timing is right, the nursery will deliver the plants just as you finish grading the area where they will be placed. Now gather them together and spread out the landscape plan.

Plant Placement

Using the plan as a guide, place the plants—still in their pots—exactly where you want them to grow. (In the case of bare-root trees or shrubs, for the moment substitute stakes.) This is the last time that you can easily change the location of plants without considerable extra effort.

Plant all the plants in an area at once. Now walk around and eye the planting critically. Remember that the plants will grow. Will that laurel crowd the boxwood hedge in a couple of years? Better move it out another 2 feet.

At first, the plantings will look thin, but have patience; a landscape needs time to grow to full maturity.

Planting

The soil has probably not been tilled where the large plants will be installed. Irrigate if it is dry; then wait a day or so for the soil to drain before planting. This will make the digging of planting holes much easier.

In general, planting holes should be as deep as the rootball, and twice as wide. Set the plant aside and dig the hole. Sprinkle fertilizer (2 tablespoons for a 1-gallon plant, ¼ cup for a 5-gallon plant, and ½ cup for a 15-gallon plant) into the hole and scratch it into the soil. Time-release fertilizer tablets may also be used (check with a local nursery).

Remove the plant from the container. Plastic cans and crimped metal cans are designed so that the plant can be knocked out without cutting the can, although straight-sided metal cans will usually have to be cut. Nurseries sell a tool for cutting cans. If many cans need to be cut, it may be worth the investment.

Since the 15-gallon cans are heavy and awkward to handle, a good way to cut them is by removing the bottom with a hatchet, before placing it in the hole. When the tree is in place, cut off the rest of the can without disturbing the tree.

Once the plant is out of the can, either loosen the roots around the outside of the rootball, or slash them with a knife across the bottom and, with three vertical cuts, up the sides. This quick pruning stimulates new root growth into the soil. This is especially important for trees; otherwise the roots circling the outside of the rootball may still be in the same

Remove the bottoms of large planting containers before placing them in the planting holes. You can use the handles of the can to move the container; this will protect the rootball of the plant if it must be lifted in and out of the hole several times. When final placement is established, cut away the remainder of the container.

place 15 years from now, choking the trunk. An alternative is to jet the rootball with a strong stream of water. This method both loosens the roots and provides water for the plant. Allow the water to drain from the hole before backfilling.

Place the plant in the hole so that the top of the rootball is level with, or even slightly above, ground level. This drains water away from the base of the plant and helps to prevent crown rot.

Tied burlap acts as a wick, drawing moisture up out of the soil. Therefore, when planting ball-and-burlap plants, place the plant in the hole, then open and fold back the top of the burlap, and bury the burlap and twine when the hole is backfilled. Many plants have their rootballs wrapped in plastic, which must be removed before planting.

When planting bare-root plants, trim off any broken or extra long roots. Place the plant in the hole, keeping the top root just below ground level. As the hole is filled, work the soil between the roots with your fingers to fill any voids.

In areas where drainage is a problem, first create a mound. Dig the planting hole in the mound so that the hole at its deepest point is roughly level with the surrounding area. This will help ensure proper runoff and better drainage, and avoid root rot and related problems.

Puddling In

No matter what type of plant is being installed, a basin must be built around it. It should be deep enough to allow one filling with a hose to saturate the entire root area, and it should be strong enough to be watered for a few weeks without falling apart.

Now fill the basin with water. As it soaks in and the backfilled soil becomes muddy, the position of the plant can be adjusted, if desired. Shake it gently to release any trapped air, and lift or turn it so that it is repositioned.

In areas where drainage is slow, reduce the size of the basin, and backfill it once the plant has settled. This helps to avoid creating areas of standing water around the plant.

Staking Trees

Drive stakes against the outside of the rootball, deep into the undisturbed soil at the bot-

Above: Do not remove the burlap wrapping of a ball-and-burlap plant. Fold it back and bury it when backfilling the hole. If plastic wrapping is used, remove before planting. Left: Create a watering basin around new plantings. Puddling in provides immediate, needed water to new plants and helps settle the surrounding soil.

tom of the hole. Don't use the stake that came in the nursery can; this is a training stake and much too light for this purpose.

Tie the trunk to the stake on the upwind side of the tree in two places: at the base of the crown and about midway along the trunk. Be sure that the tie is long enough to allow the tree to move a bit in the wind, which strengthens both the trunk and the root system. The aim is for the tree to eventually outgrow the need for the stake. Where wind is especially strong or additional support is needed, use two stakes, one on either side of the trunk. Tie the trunk securely to both stakes.

STEP 10: PLANT GROUND COVERS, BEDDING PLANTS, AND LAWN

Newly planted areas are fragile and need time to become established. Discussion of them is saved for last so that you won't be tempted to shortcut across the new lawn and damage it.

Ground Covers and Bedding Plants

These are usually planted from flats into tilled soil. Plant in rows, using triangular spacing and working away from the last-completed row so that you won't step on what has just been planted. If the soil is soft, use your hands to plant. Plant a little low, so that water will puddle at the base of each plant when it is watered. Use a watering can or a gentle stream of water from a hose. Not only does the water wet the plants, but it also settles them into the soil.

Seeding a Lawn

Level and roll the lawn area one more time to remove any footprints. Water it thoroughly if it has dried out. Spread the seeds carefully with a hand-held spreader for small lawns or a rotary spreader for large lawns. Most seeds are sown at a rate of about 1 to 2 pounds per 1,000 square feet; check with a dealer for the proper rate for the chosen seed.

Scratch the seed into the soil by raking across the lawn. A spring-toothed lawn rake does this job well. Do not pile the seed up in little piles with a back-and-forth motion, but simply drag the rake evenly from one end of the lawn to the other.

Roll with a light lawn roller (half filled with water) to press the seeds into the soil. Spread a mulch about ⅛ inch deep over the lawn. Nitrified sawdust works well. The purpose of the mulch is to keep the seeds damp, but don't make it so deep that it buries the seeds. Special spreaders are available from many nurseries to distribute the mulch. Do whatever is necessary to prevent traffic on the lawn for a few weeks.

The mulch must be kept damp for the next couple of weeks. If it dries out, newly germinated seedlings can die very quickly. Water gently by hand to avoid washing out the seeds. Once most of the seeds have germinated, let the surface of the soil dry out between

waterings—at this stage, the new seedlings are very susceptible to fungus diseases, and they will succumb more quickly if the soil is allowed to remain damp.

Mow the new lawn when it reaches 2 to 3 inches in height. If it will be kept at 2 inches high, mow as soon as it reaches 3 inches. Use a sharp mower for the first few cuttings to avoid pulling out the young plants.

Sodding a Lawn

Level and roll the ground one more time, and water it if it has dried out. Sod is cut ½ inch thick, so prepare the ground level ½ inch lower than the finished lawn will be. It is just as important to prepare the soil carefully with a sodded lawn as with a seeded one.

Have the sod delivered as close to where it will be laid as possible, even if this means removing a section of fence. In the summer the sod should not stand on the pallet any longer than one day, so plan to lay it the day it is delivered. If, however, the sod cannot be laid within a day, open up the top rolls and lay them, grass side up, over the top of the stacked pallet, letting the ends hang off. Keep the whole pallet moist. Never cover the sod with canvas or plastic.

Keep in mind the future spread and growth of plants while trying out different placement for them. Before planting, moving plants is easy, but once they are in the ground, changing their positions will be much more difficult.

Most commonly, sod is delivered in rolls that measure 18 inches wide by 6 feet long, stacked on a pallet. The delivery truck tows a forklift that will set the pallet in any area of the garden that it can reach.

Just before laying the sod, spread fertilizer on the soil and work into the top 1 inch. Usually the sod company will provide a starter fertilizer; if not, buy an appropriate fertilizer and ask someone at a nursery about proper coverage for this purpose.

Start laying the sod at the edge of a header or patio, wherever there is a straight edge to work from, or use a straight string line as a guide in laying the first row, then work outward. Work so that you are standing on the newly laid sod; otherwise your footprints will disturb the ground. Unroll a strip, then dig your fingers into the grass, and tug it toward you to snug it against the header or the edge of the adjacent strip of sod. Do not stretch it, because it will shrink slightly, and joints between strips will dry out and die. The end inside the roll of sod may have to be rolled grass side out to make it lie flat and join the next roll precisely. A standard 6-inch, sharp kitchen knife is an easy and inexpensive tool for minor trimming of sod.

Stagger the joints of the sections of sod like the bricks in a brick wall. When laying the sod on a slope, put the strips perpendicular to the slope so the rolls won't sag on the slope.

If the weather is hot and it will be more than an hour before the irrigation can be turned on, sprinkle the laid sod. The soil temperature will likely be higher than the air temperature, and therefore the roots of the grass will be especially vulnerable if the sod isn't moistened.

To make sure the joints between strips don't dry out if the weather is hot and arid, dribble sand into the cracks. This is unnecessary if the strips are placed tightly together.

Mow the newly sodded lawn when it needs it, but otherwise keep traffic off. Water daily (unless it rains) until the sod is established— usually about three weeks in warm weather. To determine whether it is established, tug gently at a corner. If the roots have grown into the soil and the new sod is knit into the ground, it is established. (For details on lawns and ground covers, see Ortho's books *All About Lawns* and *All About Ground Covers*.)

Above: Although more expensive than seed, sod produces an instant lawn.
Left: Sod will shrink slightly as it dries, so lay strips close together.
Below: A newly laid lawn is one of the most satisfying experiences of garden installation. Careful preparation and installation will assure a beautiful and trouble-free lawn.

The reward for all the hard work is a beautiful garden. A landscape will give all the more pleasure if you have designed and installed it yourself. The design of this carefully planned garden reflects the owner's taste and provides a serene, secluded retreat.

STEP 11: CLEAN UP SITE

This job won't be too extensive if the site has been cleaned up after each step. Often, extra materials (although not sod) can be returned for credit, or they can be given to neighbors.

Be thorough in cleaning. Those little piles of rock or lumber will have a tendency to take up permanent residence if they aren't removed now. A thorough cleanup gives the landscaping a professional finish. For a final touch, hose down all wood and concrete surfaces with a jet nozzle.

STEP 12: ESTABLISH AND CARE FOR PLANTS

The new plants don't really belong to the site until their roots are well established in the native soil. Until then, they are still container plants or ball-and-burlap plants, and will dry out quickly on a hot day. Check the rootballs daily—they can dry out even though the adja-

cent soil is damp. Consider using mulch to keep recently planted areas moist.

Water large plants by filling their basins with water as needed, even if there is a new sprinkler system that you are eager to use. Once the plants are established, place the plants on a regular irrigation schedule. Large plants may require extra watering from time to time, depending on soil type. If the soil is heavy, jet these plants every few weeks, or slowly flood their basins. In winter, basins can hold too much water, so they may have to be leveled.

Weeds can become a problem in newly planted areas; consider using one of the wide variety of weed-control products or-weed prevention fabrics available at many nurseries and garden centers.

Congratulations! You are the creator of a garden that will grow and mature to give you increasing satisfaction in the coming years.

U.S. Measure and Metric Measure Conversion Chart

		Formulas for Exact Measures			Rounded Measures for Quick Reference		
	Symbol	When you know:	Multiply by:	To find:			
Mass	oz	ounces	28.35	grams	1 oz		= 30 g
(Weight)	lb	pounds	0.45	kilograms	4 oz		= 115 g
	g	grams	0.035	ounces	8 oz		= 225 g
	kg	kilograms	2.2	pounds	16 oz	= 1 lb	= 450 g
					32 oz	= 2 lb	= 900 g
					36 oz	= 2¼ lb	= 1000g (1 kg)
Volume	pt	pints	0.47	liters	1 c	= 8 oz	= 250 ml
	qt	quarts	0.95	liters	2 c (1 pt)	= 16 oz	= 500 ml
	gal	gallons	3.785	liters	4 c (1 qt)	= 32 oz	= 1 liter
	ml	milliliters	0.034	fluid ounces	4 qt (1 gal)	= 128 oz	= 3¾ liter
Length	in.	inches	2.54	centimeters	⅜ in.		= 1 cm
	ft	feet	30.48	centimeters	1 in.		= 2.5 cm
	yd	yards	0.9144	meters	2 in.		= 5 cm
	mi	miles	1.609	kilometers	2½ in.		= 6.5 cm
	km	kilometers	0.621	miles	12 in. (1 ft)		= 30 cm
	m	meters	1.094	yards	1 yd		= 90 cm
	cm	centimeters	0.39	inches	100 ft		= 30 m
					1 mi		= 1.6 km
Temperature	°F	Fahrenheit	⁵⁄₉ (after subtracting 32)	Celsius	32°F		= 0°C
	°C	Celsius	⁹⁄₅ (then add 32)	Fahrenheit	212°F		= 100°C
Area	in.²	square inches	6.452	square centimeters	1 in.²		= 6.5 cm²
	ft²	square feet	929.0	square centimeters	1 ft²		= 930 cm²
	yd²	square yards	8361.0	square centimeters	1 yd²		= 8360 cm²
	a.	acres	0.4047	hectares	1 a.		= 4050 m²